# BEGINNERS

## AND

# BEYOND

For Mitchell who has supported and encouraged me in all of my endeavors.

For my sweet children who inspire me every day
to be the best mom and business owner.

For my family and friends who push me past my comfort zone
to pursue new and exciting adventures.

For my cookie family who are my forever cheerleaders.

—Joy

ISBN 13: 978-1-4621-4321-4

Published by Front Table Books, an imprint of Cedar Fort, Inc.
2373 W. 700 S., Suite 100, Springville, UT 84663
Distributed by Cedar Fort, Inc., www.cedarfort.com

Library of Congress Control Number: 2023936276

Photos of finished cookie sets taken by Samantha Vanderson
Cover design and interior layout and design by Shawnda T. Craig
Edited by Kyle Lund
Cover design © 2023 Cedar Fort, Inc.

Printed in the United States of America

10 9 8 7 6 5 4 3 2 1

Printed on acid-free paper

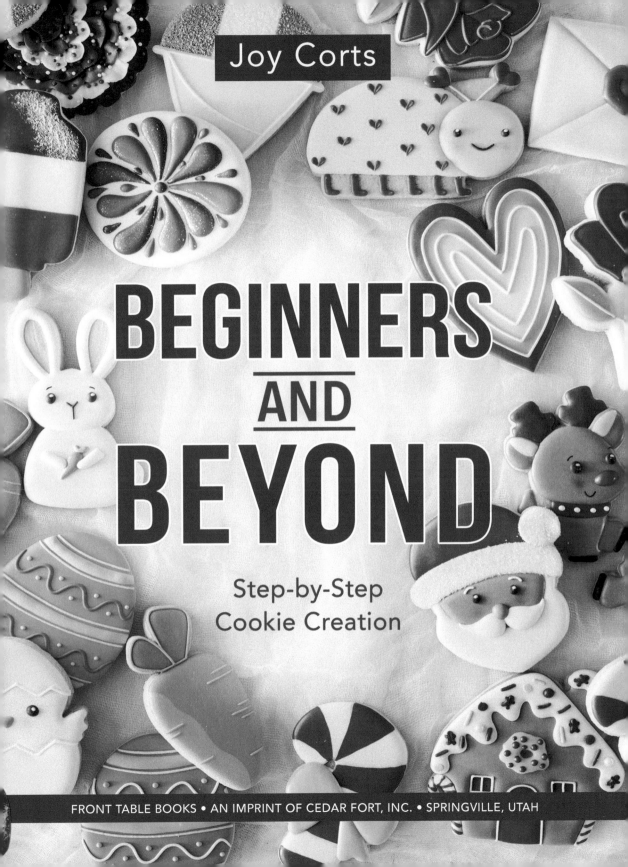

Joy Corts

# BEGINNERS
## AND
# BEYOND

Step-by-Step
Cookie Creation

FRONT TABLE BOOKS • AN IMPRINT OF CEDAR FORT, INC. • SPRINGVILLE, UTAH

# CONTENTS

MY STORY ....................................................................3

INTRO TO COOKIE DECORATING ...........................4

TOOLS: MUST HAVES AND NICE TO HAVES .............4

TIPS AND TRICKS.......................................................10

RECIPES.....................................................................19

STEP BY STEP TUTORIALS.........................................32

INDEX.......................................................................138

ABOUT THE AUTHOR.............................................140

# MY STORY

I have always been interested in baking. From making red raspberry muffins with my grandma using fresh picked raspberries from her garden to Christmas cookie platters with my mom to hand out as gifts—I loved it all. Baking has always been a way for me to relieve stress and let my creative side out.

I graduated from college in 2014 with my degree in Early Childhood Education. I got a job teaching Kindergarten that same year, which came with it's own set of stresses. I continued to bake for friends, family and coworkers to unwind, and in 2016 I was introduced to the world of cookie decorating. I had never seen such a thing and to say I was intrigued and inspired is an understatement. I made my first set of cookies for Christmas 2016 and let's just say, they were not great. I was discouraged, but I've never known myself to be a quitter. Through the gentle but firm nudging from my biggest fans (friends and family) I kept going. I was passionate about it and knew I could turn this into something special with some practice and persistence. I watched no less than one million tutorial videos and kept practicing.

In 2018 I had my first kid, my daughter Sloane, and I decided to take a year off work to spend time with her. I created a business account on Facebook and started to sell. It was mostly friends of friends but quickly spread by word of mouth through the community. By the end of that 1 year my husband and I sat down and discussed our options. Long story short, I never went back to teaching. I knew in my heart I would not get a second chance at these precious early years and wanted to spend every moment possible seeing all the "firsts." The late nights decorating can be tough but I still wouldn't go back and do it any other way! I am eternally grateful for my husband, Mitch for wholeheartedly believing in me and my capabilities.

I've spent the last 3 years growing my business, gaining new skills, and perfecting old ones. I've gotten some pretty neat orders from corporations and smaller businesses alike, but I would be remiss if I did not take a moment to mention the amazing members of my community that support me. Trusting me to make cookies for their most important events means the world. The icing on the cookie is having these people come back time and time again.

Fast forward to today, writing my very own book. So many thoughts crossed my mind when I started this journey. Why me? Am I good enough? Who even wants to listen to me blab on about my love of cookies? Pushing those negative thoughts away, I am so proud of myself for taking on this huge task to become a published author. I am so honored that you are here. I hope you learn a thing or 20 in this book and that after reading this book you fall in love with cookie decorating just like I did 6 years ago.

# INTRO TO COOKIE DECORATING

Decorated cookies have quickly become a popular staple in the baking world. For many, they are a must have at any event—from baby showers, to birthdays, to weddings, and of course the traditional holiday cookies. There is just something about these tiny pieces of art that have people oohing and aahing. It's not just the insanely intricate designs you see on social media that have people gushing, because sometimes the simple designs are the most beautiful. Whether you are a novice cookie decorator, or a seasoned professional, there are endless designs for you to try.

This book will serve as a comprehensive guide to cookie decorating. You will learn how to bake the perfect sugar cookie, make royal icing in just the right consistency, decorate over 65 designs that you can bring to most any occasion you could want cookies for, and all of the tips and tricks in between. The best part of making decorated cookies is showing them off to your friends and family. Don't be shy—show those babies off! You worked so hard over many hours, and blood, sweat and tears (ok, hopefully no blood). You may have wanted to chuck them out of your kitchen window at one point or another, but you made them with your bare hands. That is definitely something to be proud of!

Come along as we learn the ins and outs of cookie decorating! My hopes are that you learn a few new techniques, even if you are not new to the game. If you are new and are feeling the way I felt in 2016 making my first set, do not fret, I am here to help! We will go through each cookie, step by step, and I promise it won't seem so bad. Each set will start with the easiest design to build confidence, and end with the most complex design. At the end of the day, no matter what happens, you will have some delicious sugar cookies.

# TOOL MUST HAVES AND NICE TO HAVES

Getting started you really do not need to spend hundreds of dollars on all the fancy tools you may see other people using. Can I tell you a secret? When I first started, I used sandwich bags in place of piping bags and a tooth pick as a scribe. Gasp! It worked for what I needed and I am not ashamed to admit it! Below you will find a list of must haves for making and decorating cookies along with some cool tools that are available that only serve to enhance your cookie game. Once you begin your cookie decorating journey you can decide which tools you want to invest in, if any!

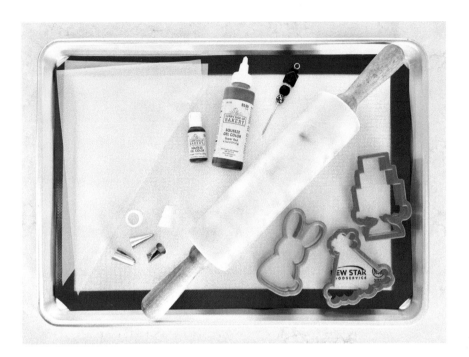

## MUST HAVES

### COOKIE SHEETS

I consider this a staple in everyone's house, but that just may be me and my lifetime of baking interest speaking. If you do not have them already, you can find them at basically any grocery or home goods store. Heck, even online. That's where we do most of our shopping now anyway, right? My personal preference is the aluminum cookie sheets as opposed to the dark coated sheets. The dark coated pans tend to brown the bottom of your cookies fast, and I am a sucker for blonde cookies.

### PARCHMENT PAPER OR SILICONE MATS

A lot of people swear by one or the other, but honestly it does not matter a ton which you use. The silicone mats are nice because they are reusable, and have you seen the price of parchment paper lately? However, if you are not baking hundreds of cookies a week, parchment paper will work just fine.

### ROLLING PIN

There are a few options when it comes to rolling pins. There are rolling pins with guide rings you stick on the ends for your preferred thickness, traditional wooden rolling pins, and my pride and joy—the marble rolling pin. Again, it's all about preference, and what you have on hand. The guided rolling pins are great for ensuring your dough is all of even thickness. The wooden rolling pin is what I used in the beginning before I stumbled upon my marble masterpiece a few years ago. Sorry wooden rolling pin, you were great and I still love you. Have I mentioned my marble rolling pin yet? She is amazing because I don't have to put very much pressure while rolling them out. The only downside is you will have to be careful that your dough is evenly rolled out and of the right thickness. After a little practice it becomes second nature.

## STAND OR HAND MIXER
An electric mixer is definitely a must have. For both the dough and the icing. Can you imagine whisking your royal icing by hand? Carpel tunnel here we come. You can choose from an electric hand mixer or a stand mixer. It is not necessary to have a stand mixer but it sure makes the process easier when you do not have to hold a hand mixer the entire time.

## MEASURING CUPS, MEASURING SPOONS AND SPATULA
If you do not already have these items, you can find them while you're at the store buying those cookie sheets!

## COOKIE CUTTERS
Careful now, collecting cookie cutters can quickly become addicting. With cookie decorating becoming increasingly popular, you can find cookie cutters in many grocery and craft stores. There is also a whole market for them online. Cookie cutters come in a few different materials. There are the traditional tin cutters that are the most cost effective. However, they are easily bendable and tend to lose their shape if you're not careful. You can also get plastic coated which are a bit more sturdy and will not rust like the tin cutters can if you do not dry them properly. 3D printed plastic cutters are the most popular options for cookies. You can find pretty much any design imaginable, and if you can't, you can have a shop make it for you online. Last up are copper cookie cutters. While they are more expensive, they are very sturdy and pretty to look at! I will be using 3D cutters from JH Cookie Co. in this book. They are an affordable and great quality cutter shop with the cutest designs! Each cookie cutter can be found on their website under the Joy of Baking tab.

If you do not have any cookie cutters you can absolutely cut your shapes out by hand using a knife. You can freehand the design, or draw your shape onto wax or parchment paper. Place the cut out image onto your rolled out dough and cut it out using a thin kitchen knife. Once the shape is cut, use your finger to smooth any rough edges around your cookie before chilling and baking.

## PIPING BAGS

If you want to forgo the trusty sandwich bags, tipless piping bags are the way to go. These bags are disposable and allow you to cut the tip as small or as big as you want it. You can find these at most craft stores, large grocery stores, and online. The best part of these bags is that you can still use tips with them! I typically do not use tips unless I am working on flowers, ruffles and the like, but when I do, I just cut a larger hole to fit the tip or coupler in. We will go over how to use tips in the step by step guide.

## PIPING TIPS & COUPLERS

Piping tips are small metal cones with various shapes on the tip that are used to create many different designs when piped. You might not use many piping tips if you use tipless piping bags, but they are necessary for designs like flowers, leaves, and ruffles. You can find piping tips at any craft store or online. I will be using a few piping tips in this book and you can find the number for each tip listed in the steps for that cookie. Couplers are used when you will be using more than one piping tip. The large part goes inside of the bag and the small ring is placed over the piping tip and twisted onto the outside of the bag.

## SCRIBE/TOOTHPICK

Scribes resemble large needles and are used to spread your icing around, while using the wet on wet technique, and to fix any boo boos you make (ie. A misplaced sprinkle etc.). Scribes or toothpicks are also used to pop air bubbles. In the next few pages you will read all about these pesky pockets of air.

## GEL FOOD COLORS

Gel food colors are used to dye your royal icing all those pretty colors. Unlike liquid food coloring, gel colors will not effect your icing consistency much (we'll go into this more later). There are several options for gel colors, but they are not all equal. When I first started I used gel colors that came in these little pots with a screw top. They were fine and did the job, but it was quite inconvenient having to scoop the color our with a tooth pick or knife. Not to mention the leaks that would happen due to taking the lid on and off repeatedly. I have enough problems when it comes to colors dying my hands, I do not need help with that! I've since discovered the magic of the squeeze bottles. Brands like Americolor, Sunny Side Up, and Chefmaster come in small and large bottles with a squeeze top that allows you to squirt one drop at a time into your icing. I still get dye on my hands occasionally because, well, that is just one of the hazards of the job, but it is a much neater process. The best part of these 3 brands is that there are a crazy amount of colors to choose from.

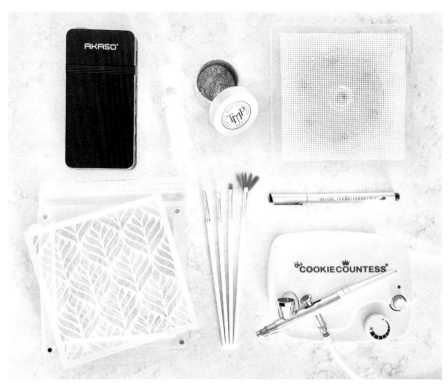

## NICE TO HAVES

### COOKIE SWIVEL

Cookie swivels are tiny turntables typically with a non-slip grip mat to decorate your cookies on. While it's not a necessary tool to have, they come in handy when you are doing detail work that requires you to turn your cookie a lot. No one, and I mean no one, likes to accidentally poke a finger into that beautiful flood icing. Sure you can scrape the icing off and start over but who wants to do that? A cookie swivel makes it easy to turn the cookie without ever having to touch it.

### AIRBRUSH MACHINE/AIRBRUSH COLORS

An airbrush machine was my first big "nice to have" tool that I received (thanks mom and dad). Let me tell you, I immediately fell in love. The options are near endless with this machine. You can airbrush the border of the cookie to give it nice dimension, airbrush a design using a stencil, or completely cover the cookie with a metallic finish. Just like with gel food colors, there are tons of color options when it comes to airbrush colors. If you are feeling bold, you can even mix them and make your own color concoction! We will go over how to airbrush using a stencil on page 34. We will be using the airbrush quite a few times in this book. If you do not have an airbrush machine, you can leave the icing as is without a pattern, or splatter with color or metallics.

## STENCILS/STENCIL HOLDER

Once you have decided to take the plunge and buy an airbrush machine and colors, you will want to invest in a stencil holder and some stencils. There are many options when it comes to stencil holders, so find what fits your needs and budget! A few of the more popular options are Stencil Genie, which is a good option at a reasonable price, and Sweet Stencil Holder, which is more expensive but great quality. Stencils can be found at a vast number of online shops. You can find a stencil in almost any design imaginable, so browse your options on google or Etsy and take your pick. Careful now, just like cookie cutters, stencils are like Pokémon cards . . . gotta catch 'em all! To organize your stencils, you can use a small binder with page protectors or a small photo album. While you do not have to do this, it is nice to be able to see all of the stencils you have without having to dig through a stack.

## PROJECTOR/STAND

Mini projectors, in cookie decorating, are small hand held devices used to project an image from your phone or computer onto your cookie. This tiny machine is my most prized cookie possession. While they can be quite costly, they are beneficial for writing specific fonts, more detailed designs like characters, and other images that may be difficult to free hand. With the purchase of your projector, you will want to also find a good stand that will hold your projector directly above the cookie you are decorating.

## EDIBLE GLITTER AND METALLICS

Who doesn't love glitter? Honestly, this mom of a clumsy 3 year old. I digress. However, when it comes to cookies I will find every chance possible to use my edible glitter. You can find them in easy to use pumps that create a nice even coat across your cookie. If by chance it does not come in a pump, you can buy empty pumps to put the glitter in. These also come in many colors. You can find these all over the internet and now at craft stores, too.

Edible metallic dust is typically mixed with grain alcohol or lemon extract to paint onto cookies. They add such a beautiful shine that it is hard not to justify this purchase. Not all metallic dusts are FDA approved, so pay close attention to the description and make your own judgment call based on what you and the people consuming your cookies are comfortable with. In this book, I use Truly Mad Plastics super gold because it has a shine that is unmatched, but it is one of those that is not FDA approved.

## EDIBLE MARKERS AND PENS

These are used to draw on fine details like faces and words, or outlining shapes. They come in sizes thick to ultra fine tip and everywhere in between. I mostly use the Tweets Cookie Connection ultra fine tip pens, which come in a variety of colors. While using edible markers and pens, you need to make sure your icing is completely dry so the tip does not poke a hole in your icing. It's a sad day when that happens. Found at the big craft stores and online, there are plenty of options for your size preference and budget. We will be using the fine tip black edible pen from Tweets Cookie Connection. If you do not have an edible pen, you can pipe those sections with black piping consistency icing!

## PAINT BRUSHES
Specifically made for use in cake and cookie decorating, paint brushes come in different sizes and shapes just like regular paint brushes. These are used for painting on cookies with watercolor (gel or airbrush colors mixed with grain alcohol), painting with metallic colors, or for brush embroidery.

## HEAT SEALER AND CELLO BAGS
Soon, you will read about storing your cookies. One option is sealing your cookies in bags. This is important to keep your cookies fresh. A heat sealer is used to melt the bag together, like a chip bag. The most popular brand is Impulse. It only takes a few seconds and creates a perfect, clean seal. You can use them on most treat bags, and you are able to adjust the heat depending on the thickness of your bag.

# TIPS AND TRICKS

# ICING CONSISTENCY

This is one of the most important parts of cookie decorating. If your icing consistency is off, it will be extremely frustrating to decorate your cookies. Let's dive in and go over the different consistencies and troubleshoot the common issues linked to each one.

## THIN FLOOD ICING
Flood icing is the icing you use once you outline the cookie, or section of the cookie, that you want to be filled. The golden number for flood icing is 7–10 seconds. Meaning if you drizzle

the icing from your spatula back into the bowl, it takes about 7–10 seconds for the icing to "melt" or settle back into the rest of the icing. To achieve the flood icing, place your stiff royal icing, straight from the mixer or storage container, into a small bowl. Add small amounts of water at a time, mix and test using the drizzle method. The amount of water needed will depend on how much icing you are thinning out. It is best to start with small amounts of water and continue adding water until you get the desired consistency. If you are working with a small amount of royal icing, you can use an eye dropper, or spray bottle to add your water. If by chance you have added too much water and your icing becomes too runny, don't panic! You can add powdered sugar into your flood icing to thicken it back up to that perfect 7–10 second consistency. I suggest adding a tablespoon at a time to avoid a back and forth of having to add water then powdered sugar. Again, icing consistency is crucial, so if you begin decorating and your icing is too thick or thin, take the time to make it right. It truly does make a world of difference. Trust me, I've tried to power through using icing that was the wrong consistency and I always regret it.

Why does consistency matter so much? When it comes to flood icing, there are a whole host of issues when you do not have the right consistency. If your icing is too thin, you may encounter icing overflowing over the edge of your cookie, even with your stiff consistency border. You also run the risk of excessive air bubbles, and color bleed (See section on color bleed: page 14 for more details). If your icing is too thick, the main issue will be that you will have a hard time getting a smooth surface. Tapping the cookie on the counter a few times, using your scribe to spread the icing around, or picking it up and shaking it may help it settle. Even then, you may be left with a wavy flood base and some tiny peaks from where you used your scribe or toothpick to even out the icing. If you notice this happening, please don't be shy and thin it out with more water. You can thank me later!

## MEDIUM FLOOD ICING
Medium Flood Icing is great for smaller sections you will be flooding. For example, leaves and petals on a flower. The best part of medium flood icing is that you do not need to pipe a thick consistency border. This icing is thick enough to stay put on your cookie, but thin enough to achieve that smooth finish on a smaller section. Aim for 12–15 second consistency with this icing. Another trick to check if it is the right consistency is to gently wiggle the bowl and see if the icing settles on its own.

## PIPING CONSISTENCY
Piping icing is best for writing on your cookies, and smaller details you may add onto your flood icing (eyes, line details, etc.). This icing never fully settles back into your bowl. If you shake the bowl it will smooth out a bit, but you should still have some soft peaks in your icing. Again, if you add in too much water, you can always thicken it back up with powdered sugar.

The goal for this icing is to create detail lines, but also be able to settle the icing smoothly with your scribe for small sections like eyes, arms, etc.

## THICK CONSISTENCY

Thick consistency is used to outline your cookie if you're using thin flood icing, or for details like flower petals, ruffles, leaves etc. This is really the easiest consistency to accomplish because in order to achieve it you have to do . . . nothing! You can use the royal icing straight from the mixer. Now let me add that if you added a little extra water into your batch of royal icing, you may need to add some powdered sugar to stiffen it up. The icing should have stiff peaks once you lift the spoon or spatula out of the bowl. In other words, you want to be able to hold the spatula up and the icing does not budge.

Consistencies will be listed in the step-by-step guide.

# COLORING ICING

Here we have another huge part of cookie decorating. Colors can truly make your cookies come to life. Scrolling on social media, it is always the sets with striking color palettes that stick out to me. From muted pastels, to vibrant rainbows, to monochromatic, to black and white—I love them all. There are an infinite number of colors and color palettes to choose from, and it can be quite overwhelming. When designing a set, I like to pull inspiration for color from the invitation and decorations. However, inspiration can really be pulled from anywhere—nature, food, clothing, possibly while aimlessly roaming the aisles at Target. Once you've selected your main color, it is time to figure out what colors you want to use along with it. I use Google images of color palettes for this one. Additionally, using two or more shades of the same color always makes for a great set. For example, bright coral and a muted coral, along with a deep forest green and a lighter sage green is a chef's kiss.

It is recommended that you use gel colors instead of the liquid food coloring, as it will not change the consistency of your icing. As you might remember from my previous obnoxiously long section, consistency is crucial. If you are making two consistencies of the same color, start with the thickest icing you will be using and add the color until it is the shade you desire. Once you've achieved that, separate however much thicker icing you will need into your piping bag and continue with your thinning process to make your next consistency.

Red and black are two of the harder colors to make. We all want those deep, rich colors, but, in cookie decorating, there is a fine line between the perfect shade and icing that is bitter and will cause color bleed. When making red and black you are aiming for almost red and almost black. Think muted versions of these colors. Once your icing is a charcoal color or light red, cover the bowl or put your icing in a piping bag. Leave your icing to sit for a few hours and let the color develop. When you come back, you should have a true red or black color. If it is still not a rich enough color at that point you can go ahead and add a little more gel color. This tip runs true for other darker colors as well, but red and black are notoriously hard to achieve.

Getting just the right color royal icing can be tricky and even 5 years later, includes a lot of trial and error. It can take a while to get the hang of, but sometimes even the best of us are throwing in a little blue here, a little black there until we are happy with the color. Icing colors will be listed at the beginning of each theme.

When it comes to determining how much icing you will need for a given set, the general rule is 1 oz per 4" cookie, .75 ounce for a 3.5" cookie, and .5 oz for a 3" cookie. I always suggest making a little bit extra because it is always best to have too much than not enough. Not much frustrates me more while decorating than running out of icing and having to try to mix more icing that exactly matches your color.  If you end up having extra icing once you're finished, you can freeze your icing in the piping bags for next time. You can also change the color for a new set if the icing color will allow it. For example, you can turn a sky blue bag of icing into navy blue.

To fill your piping bags, place the bag into a cup, tip end down, and fold the ends over the sides of the cup. If you are using a tip or coupler, cut the bag and fit the tip/coupler into the bag before filling with icing. Pour or scoop the icing into the bag. Do not overfill the bag as it will be hard to tie or clip it shut. Many a times I have disregarded my own advice, the clip busted off, and icing exploded everywhere. Do what I say not what I do, right? Remember, you can always refill your piping bag if needed. While they are disposable, I like to get as much use as I can before having to toss it. Once your bag is about half full, tie the end shut or twist and clip it with a chip clip, binder clip, really whatever you have on hand. Now you're ready to cut the tip and start the fun part!

# AIR BUBBLES

The dreaded air bubbles. Bane of my existence. Maybe a little dramatic, but they are a huge pain! Air bubbles occur during the mixing process of the royal icing. They are most likely to occur if your icing is too thin, so try to stick with that 7–10 second consistency. One way to get rid of the majority of your air bubbles is to cover the bowl of flood icing and let it sit for 20–30 minutes after mixing. This will allow the bubbles to rise to the top and you can go through with a spatula to pop them. So satisfying! Another trick you can use is pouring the icing into the bag from about 2 feet high. A lot of the bubbles will pop on their journey into the piping bag. These steps are not required, but they will save you from having to pop no less than one million bubbles later on. If, once you flood your cookie, you are still noticing some bubbles appear, use a scribe or a tooth pick and pop them.

# COLOR BLEED

Color bleed is quite frustrating. Usually, you will not notice it until the cookies have been drying awhile and it is too late. Color bleed happens for a few reasons. One being that your icing is too thin. If you are piping white flood icing next to red for example, you might experience the red color seeping or bleeding into the white if your icing is too thin. Another culprit of color bleed is if your icing is too saturated with color. Remember, those deep colors develop over time, so try not to add too much gel color in your icing to avoid that bitter taste and color bleed.

# BUTTER BLEED

I remember that fateful summer 3 years ago where it seemed like every cookie I made had butter bleed. Butter bleed is quite literally when the butter from your cookie bleeds through your royal icing. It is not cute. Fortunately, if this is happening to you, there are some solutions. once your cookies are baked, lay them in a single layer on a paper towel. If you can, let them sit for a few hours so the paper towel absorbs some of the butter from your cookie. If you are like me and lack the patience, you can decorate the cookies while on the paper towel and leave them there while they are drying. Butter bleed tends to happen in warm, humid climates. The butter in your cookie is essentially melting and the royal icing likes to suck up any moisture it can. It does not need to be an arctic tundra in your house, but try to have the air conditioner running if you can.

# DRYING AND STORAGE

With most designs there will be several dry times between steps. You want to let the flood icing have a crust on the top before moving on to create nice definition. To achieve this you can let it sit in the open air for 20–30 minutes, or you can speed the process along by placing the cookies in front of a table top fan. I use a fan for the first 30–60 minutes of the drying process so I can move through the steps quicker, and to help keep a nice shiny finish. Once your cookies are fully decorated, you will need to let them dry for at least 8 hours to be able to stack and package them. Once dry you can either store them in an airtight container, or place them in sealed bags. This step is important to keep the cookies fresh and tasty! Try not to leave them in open air for longer than 24 hours. Cookies stored properly will stay fresh for at least a week.

If you would like to keep your cookies fresh for longer than 1 week you have the option to freeze them. Place cookies in an airtight container. Layer them between wax or parchment paper if they are not sealed in bags. Then put them in the freezer. Just don't forget about them like those year old hot dogs at the bottom of your freezer! Once you are ready to take them out, leave them on the counter with the lid still on while they warm to room temperature. This will take at least 2 hours. If you open the lid too soon the condensation will make its way onto the cookies instead of staying on the outside of the container. Cookies will last up to 6 months in the freezer.

# CRATERS

Craters are tiny holes that appear once your icing dries. They most commonly appear when using thinner icing in small details, such as eyes and calligraphy writing. To avoid this, use the thickest icing possible for that area while still being able to get a smooth finish. Before you pipe that section, you can also take a thick consistency icing and make a blob or squiggle underneath that area to help hold up the icing. Try to pipe those details while the flood icing underneath is not completely dry. Remember when I said royal icing likes to suck up any moisture it can find? If your flood is completely dry, it will come for that moisture in your detail work.  Lastly, placing your cookies in front of a fan for 30–60 minutes will help it dry faster and help prevent those pesky craters.

NOW THAT YOU KNOW ALL THE INS AND OUTS OF COOKIE DECORATING, IT'S TIME FOR THE FUN PART!
LET'S DIVE IN AND DECORATE SOME BEAUTIFUL COOKIES.

# RECIPES

VANILLA SUGAR COOKIES...........................................19

LEMON CARDAMOM SUGAR COOKIES ...................21

STRAWBERRY LEMONADE SUGAR COOKIES...........23

DOUBLE CHOCOLATE CHIP SUGAR COOKIES ........25

SHORTBREAD CUTOUT COOKIES.............................27

ROYAL ICING ..........................................................29

# VANILLA SUGAR COOKIES

*A simply delicious sugar cookie that is a crowd pleaser for adults and children alike. Buttery, soft, and will not spread into unrecognizable blobs.*

• Makes roughly 24 cookies, depending on thickness and size of cookie •

## INGREDIENTS

1 cup unsalted butter, slightly softened

1½ cups granulated sugar

1 Tbsp. vanilla extract

2 eggs

1 tsp. baking powder

1 tsp. salt

4–4½ cups flour

## FLAVOR ALTERNATIVES

If you are looking to spice this recipe up, you can substitute ½ of the vanilla extract for a different flavor extract. My favorites are almond and cake batter, but feel free to play around with your favorite flavors!

## DIRECTIONS

1. Cream butter and sugar for 3–5 minutes on medium high until light and fluffy.
2. Add vanilla and eggs, one egg at a time. Scrape sides of bowl with spatula and mix again until well combined.
3. Add baking powder and salt. Mix again.
4. Add flour 1 cup at a time at a low speed. Start with 4 cups and check the dough. The dough should come together and not be too sticky along the sides of the bowl. Add the extra ½ cup of flour if the dough is still sticky. Mix until dough is combined.
5. Chill dough for 20 minutes in the freezer or 45 minutes in the fridge. The goal here is to have dough that is firm enough to keep it's shape when you transfer the cut out to the cookie sheet, but not so hard that it is difficult to roll out.
6. Roll dough to preferred thickness. I use 3/8 inch.
7. Chill the cut out cookies again in the fridge for 15–20 minutes or 5–10 minutes in the freezer. This step is important because it will ensure your cookies keep their shape in the oven.
8. Bake at 375° for 10–12 minutes or until the edges of the cookies are just starting to turn golden brown, and the tops of the cookies no longer look wet. If you roll your cookies to ¼ inch you will need to check on them a few minutes earlier. If you roll them thicker than 3/8 inches, they will likely need a longer bake time.
9. Let cool on the cookie sheet for 5 minutes and transfer to a cooling rack.
10. Let cool completely before decorating or placing them in a storage container.

# LEMON CARDAMOM SUGAR COOKIES

*A bold flavor that excites the senses! Cardamom has a fresh, lemony and minty flavor that pairs well with the lemon in this cookie.*

• Makes about 24 cookies •

## INGREDIENTS

1 cup unsalted butter,
    slightly softened

1½ cups granulated sugar

1 Tbsp. vanilla extract

Zest of 2 lemons

2 eggs

1½ tsp. cardamom

1 tsp. baking powder

1 tsp. salt

4–4½ cups flour

## FLAVOR ALTERNATIVES

Substitute orange zest for the lemon zest for another delicious flavor combination.

## DIRECTIONS

1. Cream butter and sugar for 3–5 minutes on medium high until light and fluffy.
2. Add lemon zest, vanilla, and eggs, one egg at a time. Scrape sides of bowl with spatula and mix again until well combined.
3. Add cardamom, baking powder, and salt. Mix again.
4. Add flour, 1 cup at a time, at a low speed. Start with 4 cups and check the dough. The dough should come together and not be too sticky along the sides of the bowl. Add the extra ½ cup of flour if the dough is still sticky. Mix until dough is combined.
5. Chill dough for 20 minutes in the freezer or 45 minutes in the fridge.
6. Roll dough to preferred thickness and cut out your shapes.
7. Chill the cut out cookies again in the fridge for 15–20 minutes or 5–10 minutes in the freezer. This step is important because it will ensure your cookies keep their shape in the oven.
8. Bake at 375° for 10–12 minutes or until the edges of the cookies are just starting to turn golden brown, and the tops of the cookies no longer look wet or shiny. Bake shorter or longer, depending on the thickness you rolled out your cookies. If you roll your cookies to ¼ inch you will need to check on them a few minutes earlier. If you roll them thicker than 3/8 inches, they will likely need a longer bake time.
9. Let cool on the cookie sheet for 5 minutes and transfer to a cooling rack.
10. Let cool completely before decorating or placing them in a storage container.

# STRAWBERRY LEMONADE SUGAR COOKIES

*Perfect for summer, these fresh and fruity bites of joy are ready for an invitation to your next cookout.*

• Makes about 24 cookies •

## INGREDIENTS

1 cup unsalted butter, slightly softened

1 cup granulated sugar

2 tsp. vanilla extract

1 tsp. lemon extract

1 oz. freeze dried strawberries, ground into powder (about ½ cup powder)

Zest of 2 lemons

2 eggs

1 tsp. baking powder

1 tsp. salt

4–4½ cups flour

## FLAVOR ALTERNATIVES

You can use freeze dried raspberries in place of the strawberries for a fun twist. Who doesn't love raspberry lemonade?

Optional: Replace 1 Tbsp water per cup of royal icing with lemon juice for an extra citrus flavor.

## DIRECTIONS

1. Cream butter and sugar for 3–5 minutes on medium high until light and fluffy.

2. Add strawberry powder, lemon zest, and vanilla. Mix.

3. Add eggs, one at a time. Scrape sides of bowl with spatula and mix again until well combined.

4. Add baking powder and salt. Mix again.

5. Add flour 1 cup at a time at a low speed. Start with 4 cups and check the dough. The dough should come together and not be too sticky along the sides of the bowl. Add the extra ½ cup of flour if the dough is still sticky. Mix until dough is combined.

6. Chill dough for 20 minutes in the freezer or 45 minutes in the fridge.

7. Roll dough to preferred thickness and cut out shapes.

8. Chill the cut out cookies again in the fridge for 15–20 minutes or 5–10 minutes in the freezer.

9. Bake at 375° for 10–12 minutes or until the edges of the cookies are just starting to turn golden brown, and the tops of the cookies no longer look wet. If you prefer crunchier cookies, bake them an extra minute or 2 until the edges are all golden brown.

10. Let cool on the cookie sheet for 5 minutes and transfer to a cooling rack.

11. Let cool completely before decorating or placing them in a storage container.

# DOUBLE CHOCOLATE CHIP SUGAR COOKIES

*This decadent cookie is my twist on a traditional chocolate sugar cookie. Because the more chocolate the better! Perfect for your holiday baking.*

• Makes about 24 cookies •

## INGREDIENTS

1 cup unsalted butter, slightly softened

1½ cups granulated sugar

1 tsp. vanilla extract

2 eggs

2/3 cup Dutch process cocoa powder (the higher quality the better!)

1 tsp. baking powder

1 tsp. salt

3–3½ cups flour

¾ cup mini chocolate chips

## FLAVOR ALTERNATIVES

Leave out the chocolate chips for a more traditional chocolate sugar cookie

Add ¾ tsp peppermint extract into your royal icing to make the ultimate peppermint bark Christmas cookie!

## DIRECTIONS

1. Cream butter and sugar for 3–5 minutes on medium high until light and fluffy.
2. Add vanilla and eggs, one at a time. Scrape sides of bowl with spatula and mix again until well combined.
3. Add cocoa powder and mix until combined.
4. Add baking powder and salt. Mix again.
5. Add flour, 1 cup at a time, at low speed. Start with 3 cups and check the dough. The dough should come together and not be too sticky along the sides of the bowl. Add the extra ½ cup of flour if the dough is still sticky. Mix until dough is combined.
6. Add chocolate chips and mix on lowest setting or by hand until evenly dispersed. It is important to use mini chocolate chips so that the shapes are easier to cut out. Once upon a time I used regular chocolate chips and I was very sad.
7. Chill dough for 20 minutes in the freezer or 45 minutes in the fridge.
8. Roll dough to preferred thickness and cut out shapes.
9. Chill the cut out cookies again in the fridge for 15–20 minutes or 5–10 minutes in the freezer.
10. Bake at 375° for 10–12 minutes, or until the edges of the cookies are just starting to turn golden brown and the tops of the cookies no longer look wet. If you prefer crunchier cookies, bake them an extra minute or 2 until the edges are all golden brown.
11. Let cool on the cookie sheet for 5 minutes and transfer to a cooling rack.
12. Let cool completely before decorating or placing them in a storage container.

# SHORTBREAD CUTOUT COOKIES

*Not only are these egg free for those with allergies, they absolutely melt in your mouth. I dare you not to eat the whole batch!*

• Makes about 18 cookies •

## INGREDIENTS

1 cup unsalted butter

1 cup powdered sugar

1 tsp. vanilla extract

3 cups flour

1 tsp. salt

## FLAVOR ALTERNATIVES

Try out some flavor variances by adding 1 tsp of almond or cake batter extract.

## DIRECTIONS

1. With a paddle attachment, mix butter until creamed.
2. Add vanilla, powdered sugar, and salt. Mix. Scrape down sides of bowl and mix until combined.
3. Add flour, 1 cup at a time, until combined.
4. Knead dough into a ball and wrap in plastic wrap or parchment paper.
5. Chill dough for 20 minutes in the freezer or 45 minutes in the fridge.
6. This dough has a tendency to be a bit more crumbly than other recipes, so you will need to knead the dough until it forms a ball. Roll dough to preferred thickness and cut out shapes.
7. Bake at 375° for 10–12 minutes, or until the edges of the cookies are just starting to turn golden brown and the tops of the cookies no longer look wet. If you prefer crunchier cookies, bake them an extra minute or 2 until the edges are all golden brown.
8. If there was any air in your dough it might come out of the oven with domes or bubbles on top. As soon as you take it out of the oven, use the back of a spoon to flatten the tops.
9. Let cool on the cookie sheet for 5 minutes and transfer to a cooling rack.
10. Let cool completely before decorating or placing them in a storage container.

# ROYAL ICING

*We've finally come to the good part. The magical icing you will use to make cookie art. The super sweet taste of royal icing (it is almost pure sugar after all) is the perfect balance to that buttery sugar cookie.*

• Makes about 3 cups of icing •

## INGREDIENTS

4 cups powdered sugar

3 Tbsp. meringue powder*

1 tsp clear vanilla extract

6–7 Tbsp. water

1 Tbsp. corn syrup
(optional)

## FLAVOR ALTERNATIVES

Substitute clear almond flavoring (almond extract has oil and won't bode well with your icing) for half of the vanilla if you prefer the almond taste.

## DIRECTIONS

1. Add powdered sugar, meringue powder, clear vanilla, and water into mixer. Start your mixer on the lowest setting so you do not have an explosion of powdered sugar. Turn the mixer up to medium–high for 3–5 minutes. The icing should be bright white, light and fluffy, and have stiff peaks. If your icing is starting to clump and no longer appear smooth, turn the mixer off. You do not want to over mix your icing as it will resemble a sponge when it dries on your cookie.

2. Add corn syrup and mix until combined. Corn syrup helps to keep the icing shiny and makes for a softer bite when it dries. Your icing will be just fine if you want to skip this step!

3. You are ready to thin out your icing, if needed, and decorate! Store icing you are not using in a covered container to prevent it from drying out. Icing lasts for months in the fridge if stored properly (airtight container). You can also freeze royal icing. Pull it out to thaw for a few hours before you use it.

NOTE: *meringue powder is essentially dried egg whites and is a key ingredient in royal icing. The meringue powder is what makes your icing dry hard. If there is an egg allergy and you want an egg free option to go with my shortbread recipe, there are vegan meringue powder options found online!

# STEP-BY-STEP TUTORIALS

OUTLINING AND FLOODING ...............................................32

AIRBRUSHING .................................................................34

WEDDING ......................................................................37
RING 37, CAKE 38, DRESS 39, MONOGRAM 40

BABY SHOWER ................................................................43
BIB 43, BABY FEET 44, PAJAMAS 45, RATTLE 46

BIRTHDAY.......................................................................49
CANDLE 49, BALLOONS 50, PARTY HAT 51, CAKE 52

VALENTINE'S DAY.............................................................55
ENVELOPE 55, HEART 56, LOVE BUG 57, ROSE 58

ST. PATRICK'S DAY ..........................................................61
FOUR LEAF CLOVER 61, LEPRECHAUN BEARD 62,
POT O' GOLD 63, RAINBOW 64

EASTER..................................................................67
    CARROT 67, CHICK 68, EASTER EGG 69, BUNNY 70

MOTHER'S DAY....................................................73
    FLOWER POT 73,  LEAF 1 & LEAF 2 74, FLOWER 75,
    FLOWER CLUSTER 76

FATHER'S DAY.......................................................79
    LETTUCE 79, CHEESE 80, BURGER 80,
    TOP & BOTTOM BUN 81, TOMATO 82

4TH OF JULY .........................................................85
    SNOW CONE 85, BOMB POP 86, FLAG 87, FIREWORK 88

HALLOWEEN ........................................................91
    BAT 91, GHOST 92, JACK-O'-LANTERN 93, CAULDRON 94

THANKSGIVING....................................................97
    PUMPKIN PIE 97, CHERRY PIE 98, PECAN PIE 99, TURKEY 100

CHRISTMAS.........................................................103
    CANDY CANE 103, SANTA 104, REINDEER 105,
    GINGERBREAD HOUSE 106

NEW YEARS .........................................................109
    NYE BALL 109, CLOCK 110, CHAMPAGNE BOTTLE 111,
    "HAPPY NEW YEAR" 112

WINTER ...............................................................115
    TREE 115, SNOWMAN 116, SNOWFLAKE 117, HAT 118

SPRING ................................................................121
    FLOWERS 121, BIRD 122, WATERING CAN 123, SUN HAT 124

SUMMER ..............................................................127
    SUN 127, WATERMELON 128, SANDCASTLE 129,
    ICE CREAM 130

FALL.....................................................................133
    PUMPKIN 133, MUG 134, SUNFLOWER 135, SWEATER 136

1. PREPARING YOUR PIPING BAG: If you are using a tipless bag, cut the very tip of the bag with the seam on the side. Make sure you cut it straight across, otherwise your icing will curl when it comes out of the bag. If you would like to use tips, tip #1 and #2 are both good options.

2. OUTLINE: Using your stiff consistency icing, put the tip of the bag directly onto the cookie. When you begin to squeeze, lift the bag and let the icing fall onto the cookie as you outline. This will give you a nice clean line.

3. OUTLINE CHANGING DIRECTIONS: If you are doing shapes that require you to change directions with your outline (flowers, sun, etc.), slowly release pressure from your piping bag as you touch the tip back down at the turning point. Lift the piping bag back up as you continue piping the rest of the outline.

4. FLOODING: Using your thin flood consistency icing, begin by placing your tip at any point along the outline. You may also start in the middle and work your way out if you are feeling adventurous. Squeeze the piping bag gently so there is a nice flow of icing and pipe along the outline of your cookie. The tip of your bag should be very close to the cookie, but not touching it.

5. FLOODING: Continue working your way around the cookie until you get to the middle and the cookie is completely covered in royal icing.

STEP 1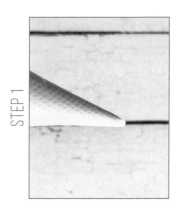

STEP 2

STEP 3

STEP 4

STEP 5

6.  GAPS: Use the tip of your bag or your scribe to fill any gaps in your icing.

7.  AIR BUBBLES: Use your scribe to pop any air bubbles. Whether you work your way from the outside to the inside, the inside to the outside, or from side to side, it really does not matter much—you will have a beautiful flood however you choose to do it!

STEP 6

STEP 7

## NOTES

# AIRBRUSHING

1.  Outline and flood your cookie. Let dry for at least 2 hours, or until completely dry.

2.  Place your selected stencil into your stencil holder. Make sure the stencil is flat. If your stencil is bowed at all, it will cause underspray. This means that the airbrush color will make its way underneath the solid sections of your stencil and cause a color shadow around the pattern. It is also important that you use enough icing while flooding and make sure the flood is completely smooth to avoid underspray.

3.  Hold your airbrush gun about 6 inches above the cookie, and as close to vertical as possible without the color spilling. This will prevent the air pressure from lifting up the stencil and causing underspray.

4.  If you want a more saturated airbrush color, add several light layers of color, allowing them to dry for a few seconds between passes. Adding too much too fast will cause the color to separate a bit on the cookie and the color won't be smooth.

5.  Carefully lift the stencil straight up off of the cookie. Lifting it off at an angle could cause the stencil to smudge your fresh airbrush color.

STEP 1

STEP 2

STEP 3

STEP 4

STEP 5

# NOTES

# WEDDING

ICING COLORS: white, dusty blue (navy blue with a touch of black)

COOKIE SHAPES: ring, cake, dress, monogram

## RING

1. Outline the entire cookie with white thick consistency icing and flood with white thin flood icing. Let dry for 30 minutes.

2. It is best to do this next step while the flood icing is just crusted to prevent cratering on the band. Outline the band and diamond prongs with white thick consistency icing. You may choose to add an inner line of thick consistency icing at this point to help with cratering. Immediately fill in this section with white medium flood consistency icing.

3. Outline the diamond with white thick consistency icing and fill in with your white medium flood icing. Dry in front of a fan for 30 minutes to prevent cratering of the diamond and band.

4. Use white piping consistency icing to outline the border of your diamond. Pipe a line from the two outer corners, and complete it with your triangular shapes.

5. Once the band and prongs of your cookie have dried for at least 2 hours, use your favorite edible gold dust mixed with grain alcohol or edible gold paint to paint the band.

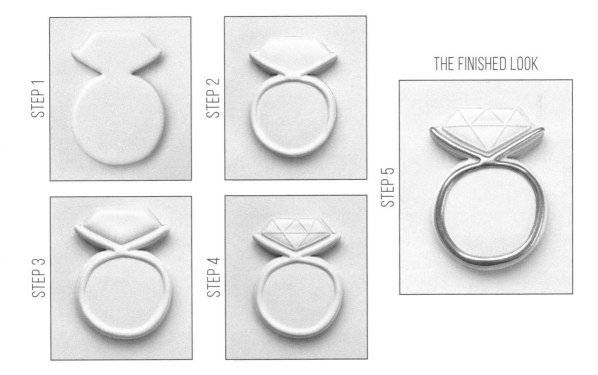

STEP 1

STEP 2

STEP 3

STEP 4

THE FINISHED LOOK

STEP 5

# CAKE

1. Outline the cake stand with white thick consistency icing and fill it in with white medium flood icing.

2. Outline and fill in the middle tier of the cake with your white thick consistency and medium flood icing. Let dry for 2 hours, with the first 15–20 minutes in front of a fan.

3. Outline and fill in the top tier of your cake with white thick consistency and medium flood icing. Paint the cake stand with your edible gold.

4. Add horizontal lines to the middle tier using white piping consistency icing.

5. Outline and fill in the bottom tier with white piping consistency icing.

6. Using your scribe or toothpick, swirl the icing in on the bottom tier immediately after piping. Don't be afraid to keep playing with it until you get your desired look.

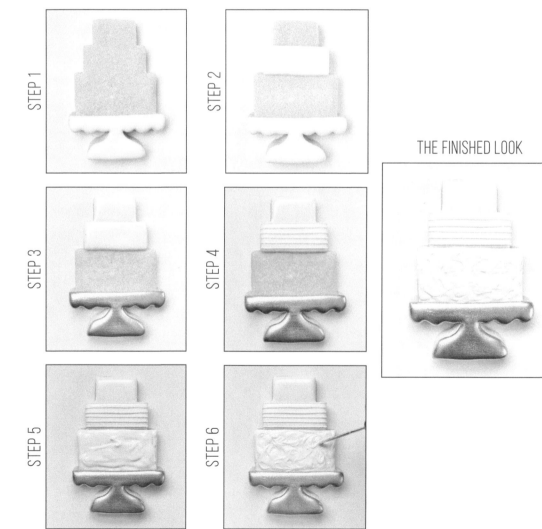

THE FINISHED LOOK

# DRESS

1. Outline and flood the bust of the dress with white medium flood icing. Let dry for 15 minutes.

2. Turning your cookie upside down and, starting at the bottom corner of the dress, use tip #103 to pipe the ruffles. Think of them as tiny rainbows. Start with the tip touching your cookie at a slight angle. As you begin piping, slightly lift the bag up just enough so the tip is no longer touching the cookie.

3. As you work your way across the cookie, make your tiny rainbows by moving the bag up and down as you move from one side to the other.

4. Using the same technique, pipe the next row of ruffles so that the two layers are slightly overlapping.

5. Continue this process until your reach the bust of the dress.

6. If there is any bare cookie showing, use your scribe tool to maneuver the icing to close the gaps.

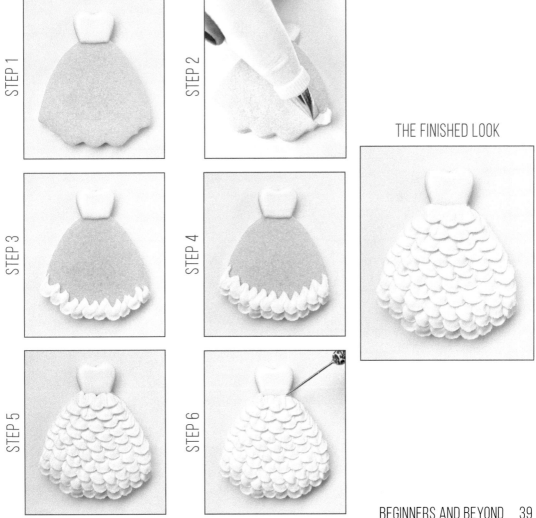

STEP 1

STEP 2

STEP 3

STEP 4

STEP 5

STEP 6

THE FINISHED LOOK

1. Outline your cookie with white thick consistency icing and flood with white thin flood icing. Let this cookie dry completely for 6–8 hours before moving on to the next step.

2. To make your watercolor, start with a mixture of half grain alcohol and half water. Add your navy gel color or navy airbrush color and ensure it is mixed well. You will also need a mixture of just grain alcohol and water to use as a base coat. Coat the entire cookie with the grain alcohol and water mixture using a paint brush.

3. Immediately dab on several spots using your color mixture and a new paint brush.

4. You will then use your first paint brush and drop on more of your clear mixture.

5. Use your second paint brush to spread the color around until you are satisfied with the look. You want to make sure you are doing all of these steps as quickly as possible so the color doesn't absorb into the cookie and leave funny looking polka dots. *An alternative to this watercolor effect is to simply flood the cookie in a solid color of your choice.

STEP 1

STEP 2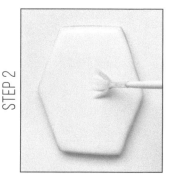

STEP 3

STEP 4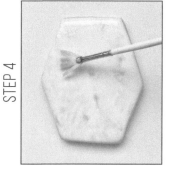

STEP 5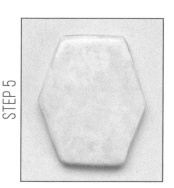

6.  Once your watercolor has dried, outline and fill an oval in the center of your cookie using white thick consistency icing and white medium flood icing. Let dry in front of a fan for 20 minutes.

7.  Using dusty blue piping consistency icing, outline the letter of your choosing onto the oval. As a rule of thumb, the thicker sections of a letter are on the down stroke. Google is a great resource for finding the perfect font. You can also print out the letter and practice tracing it with your icing before piping on the cookie.

8.  Using dusty blue medium flood icing, fill the wide "down stroke" section of your letter.

9.  Dry in front of your fan for the first 30 minutes to prevent cratering.

STEP 6

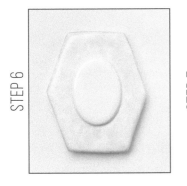

STEP 7

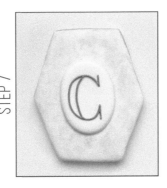

THE FINISHED LOOK

STEP 8

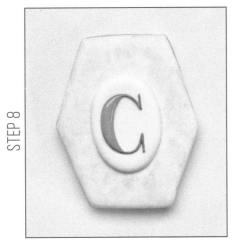

# BABY SHOWER

ICING COLORS: white, light green (green and a touch of black), dark green
(more green and a tiny bit more black)

COOKIE SHAPES: bib, baby feet, pajamas, rattle

## ———— BIB ————

1. Outline one side of the scallops using white piping consistency icing. Start with only half of the cookie so the icing doesn't dry out too much as you are working on the lace technique. (tip: cut the hole of the bag a bit larger so there is enough icing to drag with your paint brush) Using a small paintbrush, drag the icing towards the middle of the cookie. You do not need to drag in too far as you will be covering the majority of the cookie with icing.

2. Repeat this process on the other half of the cookie.

3. Outline and flood the bib with dark green thick consistency and thin flood icing, leaving enough room on the sides and bottom so the lace is visible. Let dry for 20 minutes.

4. Add the 3 dot pattern using light green piping consistency icing.

STEP 1

STEP 2

THE FINISHED LOOK

STEP 3

STEP 4

# BABY FEET

1. Outline the cookie with white thick consistency icing and flood with white thin flood icing. Let dry completely for 6–8 hours.

2. Apply a thick line of light green thick consistency icing to one side of your cookie.

3. Use your scraper tool or the backside of a butter knife to scrape the icing across the cookie. Don't be afraid to go back and scrape a few more times to create a layered effect.

4. Pipe bean shapes in the middle of your cookie using dark green medium flood icing.

5. Using the same icing, add 5 dots to each foot to create the toes.

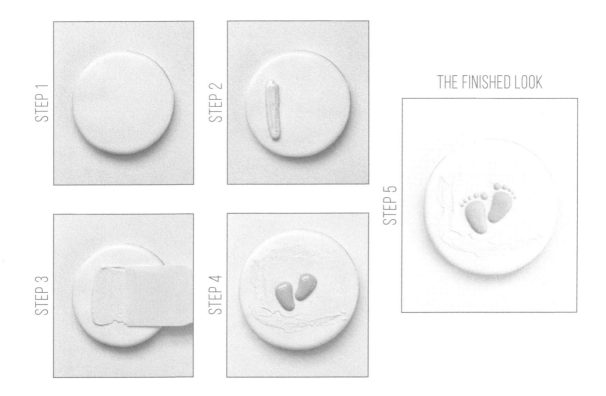

THE FINISHED LOOK

STEP 1
STEP 2
STEP 3
STEP 4
STEP 5

# PAJAMAS

1. Outline and flood the left side of the cookie with light green thick consistency icing and light green thin flood icing. Use a curved line on the chest section. Let dry for at least 2 hours.

2. Airbrush a green leaf design. This is the botanical leaves stencil from Killer Zebras.

3. Outline and flood the right side using your dark green thick consistency icing and dark green thin flood icing. Let dry completely for 6–8 hours.

4. Add some piping consistency dark green icing onto the right side of your cookie.

5. Use a paintbrush to dab the icing across the entire dark green section to create a fuzzy effect.

6. Pipe the buttons using dark green piping consistency icing.

STEP 1

STEP 2

STEP 3

STEP 4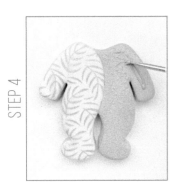

STEP 5

THE FINISHED LOOK

STEP 6

# RATTLE

1. Outline the top of the rattle with white thick consistency icing and fill with white flood icing. It is important to use a thin flood so the icing will settle nicely after the next step.

2. Pipe alternating dark and light green lines with flood consistency icing. Use the border as a guide.

3. Immediately go in with your scribe and drag the tip of the scribe through the middle of the lines. Go around the circle 2 times.

4. Outline and flood the bottom of the rattle with dark green medium flood consistency icing.

5. Pipe the handle of the rattle with white thick consistency icing. You do not need to extend it all the way to the top as that will be covered by the bow.

6. Outline and flood the loop sections of the bow with light green icing. I like to use a thick outline and medium flood to ensure the shape stays how I piped it. Let dry for 15 minutes.

7. Outline and flood the tails of the bow with the same icing. Let dry for 15 minutes.

8. Add a border and "loop" on the bow using light green piping consistency icing.

9. Outline the center of the bow with light green thick consistency icing. Add a dollop to the inside of this section to help prevent cratering.

10. Fill in the circle with light green medium flood icing.

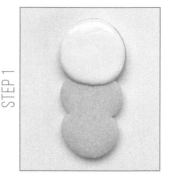
STEP 1

STEP 2

STEP 3

STEP 4

STEP 5

STEP 6

STEP 7

STEP 8

STEP 9

THE FINISHED LOOK

STEP 10

# BIRTHDAY

ICING COLORS: white, coral (light pink with a tiny amount of yellow), blue, green, black

COOKIE SHAPES: candle, balloons, party hat, cake

## CANDLE

1. Outline and fill three sections of the candle using green medium flood icing. Make sure to leave a bare section in between each so we can create that nice dimension. Let dry for 20 minutes.

2. Outline and fill in the remaining three sections with green medium flood icing.

3. Pipe the flame onto the candle using white medium flood icing. Let dry for 20 minutes.

4. Pipe the wick onto the flame of the candle using black piping consistency icing.

STEP 1    STEP 2

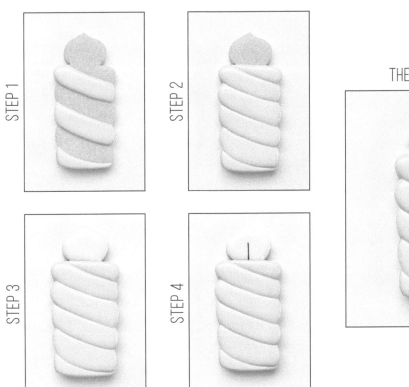

STEP 3    STEP 4

THE FINISHED LOOK

# BALLOONS

1. Outline with white thick consistency icing, and flood with white thin flood icing. Let dry for 30 minutes.

2. Pipe the bottom right balloon first using blue medium flood icing. It will be easier to shape the balloons around this one as this is the only full balloon. Let dry for 15 minutes.

3. Pipe the bottom left balloon next using green medium flood icing. Make sure the balloons are touching. Add the tail of the blue balloon using your blue medium flood icing. Let dry for 15 minutes.

4. Pipe the top balloon using coral medium flood icing. Use your scribe tool if necessary to drag the icing to a point where all 3 balloons meet. Add the tail of the green balloon using your green medium flood icing.

5. Use thick black icing to add the ribbons of your balloons. Start at the balloon and work your way to the bottom. It is important to lift the piping bag up at least half an inch above your cookie once you start piping and let the icing fall onto the cookie to create the loops.

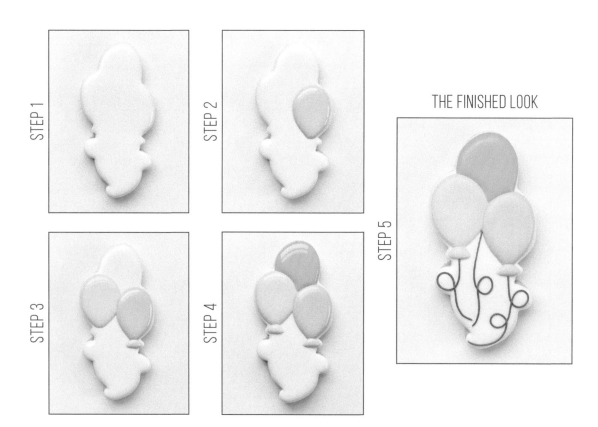

STEP 1

STEP 2

STEP 3

STEP 4

STEP 5

THE FINISHED LOOK

# PARTY HAT

1. Outline the cookie with green medium flood icing. Pipe diagonal lines, alternating thick and thin sections. Fill in the thick sections with your green icing.

2. Immediately fill in the thin sections with blue medium flood consistency icing. Let dry for 30 minutes. Pipe thin lines using blue piping consistency icing along the borders of the blue stripes.

3. Outline and fill the top and bottom of the hat with coral piping consistency icing.

4. Use your scribe tool to swirl the icing until you are happy with the look.

5. As soon as you are done swirling the icing, sprinkle white nonpareils onto the coral icing.

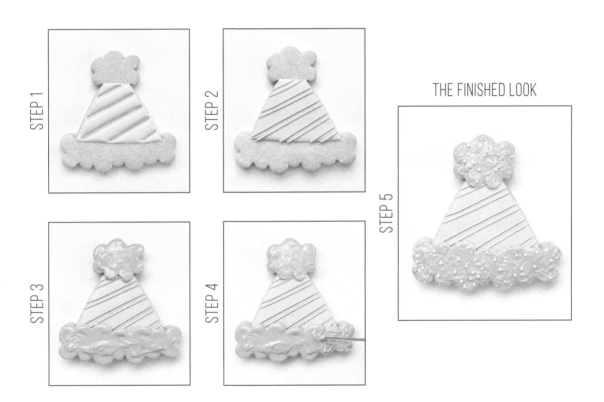

STEP 1

STEP 2

STEP 3

STEP 4

STEP 5

THE FINISHED LOOK

# CAKE

1. Use medium flood blue, green, and coral icing to outline and fill the cake and candle sections. Let dry for 15 minutes.

2. Add the flame of the candle with white medium flood icing. Let dry for 10 minutes and add a thin line for the wick using black piping consistency icing.

3. Making your own sprinkles is a great way to color match with your set. Use thick consistency icing of each color in your set and pipe straight lines onto parchment paper. Let dry for at least an hour, and break them up using a knife or your scraper tool. So easy and so fun!

4. Outline the frosting section with white thick consistency icing. Add the drips by letting the icing fall onto the cookie while moving the bag up and down as you move from one side to the other. Pipe some filler on the inside of this section with the same icing to prevent cratering.

5. Flood this section with white medium flood icing.

6. While the icing is still wet, sprinkle your homemade sprinkles onto the white icing, or place them one by one for a more uniform look.

STEP 1

STEP 2

STEP 3

THE FINISHED LOOK

STEP 4

STEP 5

STEP 6

# NOTES

# VALENTINE'S DAY

ICING COLORS: white, pink, lighter pink and lightest pink (varying amounts of light pink gel color), red, green (green with a touch of black gel color)

COOKIE SHAPES: envelope, heart, love bug, rose

## ENVELOPE

1. Using white thick consistency icing, pipe 2 diagonal lines connecting all 4 corners. It should look like an X on your cookie. Pipe the border on the top and bottom to make 2 triangles. Flood the triangles with white thin flood icing. Let dry for 15 minutes.

2. Pipe a border on the sides of the cookie using white thick consistency icing. Flood the remaining 2 sections with white thin flood icing. Let dry for 20 minutes.

3. Pipe a small heart at the center of your cookie using red medium flood consistency icing. The heart does not need to be perfect here. Let dry for 10 minutes.

4. Using that same red icing, pipe an outline of a heart on top of the one you just made. Then pipe a wavy circle around the heart. This can be any random wavy lines since wax seals are never perfect. Fill in with your red icing.

5. Use your airbrush gun filled with light pink airbrush color to airbrush the border of your cookie and the seams of your envelope.

STEP 1

STEP 2

THE FINISHED LOOK

STEP 3

STEP 4

STEP 5

# HEART

1. Using red medium flood icing, outline the entire cookie. Add another outline about a centimeter in from the cookie. Fill in the section with the same red icing.

2. Immediately add another line another centimeter in from the red section using pink medium flood icing, and fill in this section. This technique is called wet on wet (just as we did with the baby rattle) and piping sections one right after the other will create a smooth finish.

3. Pipe another line a centimeter in from the pink section using a lighter pink medium flood icing and fill in.

4. Using your lightest pink color, fill in the rest of the middle of the heart. Let dry for 30 minutes.

5. Using piping consistency icing of all 3 of your pink shades, pipe a line along the borders of each color. Match the piping consistency icing to each of your 3 pink shades. Don't forget to hold the icing bag about an inch above the cookie and let the icing fall to create nice and neat lines.

STEP 1  STEP 2  THE FINISHED LOOK  STEP 5  STEP 3  STEP 4

# LOVE BUG

1. Outline and flood a circle for the head using your lighter pink medium flood icing. Let dry for 15 minutes.

2. Outline and flood the body of your love bug using your lightest pink medium flood consistency icing. Let dry for 20 minutes.

3. Pipe tiny hearts onto the body using red piping consistency icing. Squeeze the bag to create the rounded top and as you slowly release pressure drag the bag to the tip at the bottom. Repeat on the other side of the heart, finishing at the same point you ended the first side.

4. Add the antennae using lighter pink piping consistency icing.

5. Add larger hearts at the top of the antennae using red piping consistency icing.

6. Add 6 "L" shaped feet along the bottom using your red piping consistency icing.

7. Complete this cutie by adding 2 eyes and a mouth using black piping consistency icing. Add a small white dot to each eye using white piping consistency icing. Airbrush light pink dots for cheeks. You may also use pink luster dust and swirl them on with a small paintbrush once dry.

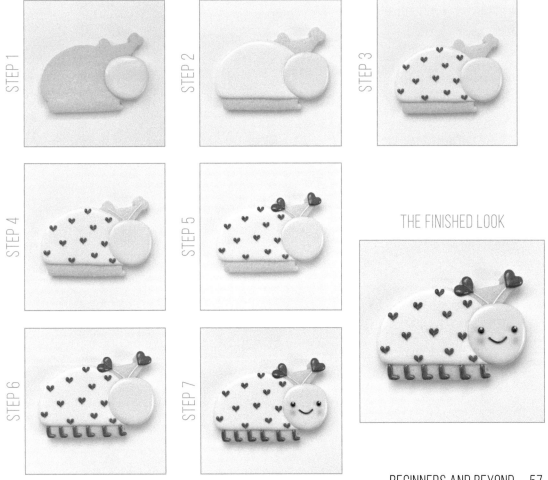

STEP 1  STEP 2  STEP 3  STEP 4  STEP 5  STEP 6  STEP 7

THE FINISHED LOOK

# ROSE

*NOTE: This cookie has quite a lot of drying times, but if you are making several of this shape you can work on one step at a time on all of the cookies. Once you are finished with the last cookie it will be time to move onto the next step on your first cookie!*

1. Outline entire cookie with white thick consistency icing and flood with white thin flood icing. Let dry for 30 minutes.

2. Add a stem and leaf outlines using green piping consistency icing.

3. Fill in the leaves with green medium flood consistency icing.

4. Pipe a small circle towards the top of the flower using red medium flood icing. Let dry for 10 minutes.

5. Add a small half heart shape on the right side of the circle. The best part of this cookie is these shapes do not have to be identical and it will still turn out beautiful. Let dry for 10 minutes.

6.  Pipe the next section on the left side, making sure the icing completely touches the 2 previous sections. Let dry for 10 minutes.

7.  Pipe a circle (circle is a loose term here) directly underneath these shapes. Let dry for 10 minutes.

8.  Pipe the large petal, making sure to touch the circle you piped in the last step. Let dry for 10 minutes.

9.  Pipe the next small petal and use your scribe to drag the icing to where it is touching the other sections. Let dry for 10 minutes.

10. Add the bottom right petal right along side the large petal.

11. Outline the top right petal and fill in the entire section. Use your scribe to get into any tight spaces if needed.

12. Outline the top left petal. Bring your outline down to touch the large petal. Fill in this section and let dry for 10 minutes.

13. Complete the rose by outlining and filling in the remaining petal. Let dry for 10 minutes.

14. Using green piping consistency icing, add lines down the center of each leaf. Using red piping consistency icing, add lines along the border of each petal. Finish the center circle with a curved line into the center to create a rose bud effect. Whew, that was a process! But you did it and I bet you made one beautiful cookie.

STEP 10

STEP 11

STEP 12

STEP 13

THE FINISHED LOOK

STEP 14

# ST. PATRICK'S DAY

ICING COLORS: white, red, orange, yellow, green, blue, violet, black

COOKIE SHAPES: four leaf clover, leprechaun beard, pot o' gold, rainbow

## —————— FOUR LEAF CLOVER ——————

1. Outline the entire cookie with green thick consistency icing and flood with green thin flood icing. Let dry for at least 2 hours.

2. Airbrush diagonal stripes using green airbrush color. This stencil is the small stripes stencil from Killer Zebras.

3. Airbrush diagonal stripes in the opposite direction to create the gingham effect.

4. Using green piping consistency icing, pipe along the border adding little loops at the center of each leaf.

STEP 1  STEP 2  STEP 3  STEP 4  STEP 5

THE FINISHED LOOK

# LEPRECHAUN BEARD

1.  Before you bake this cookie, take a lollipop stick and stick it through the center of the cookie. Make sure that the stick is not poking out of the front or back of the cookie to ensure it doesn't fall off the stick once baked. Place the stick most of the way up into the cookie for even more stability. Leave the stick out if you do not want to make cookie pops!

2.  Outline and flood one side of the mustache using orange medium flood icing. Let dry for 10 minutes.

3.  Outline and flood the other half of the mustache using the same icing. Let dry for 10 minutes.

4.  Outline and flood the beard of the cookie. Use your scribe to drag the icing into the middle of the mustache. Let dry for 15 minutes.

5.  Using orange piping consistency icing, add 2 lines to each side of the mustache using the curve of the cookie as a guide. Add lines with curls at the bottom onto the beard. Once you finish you can hold them up to your face for a little giggle. This is a crowd pleaser for kids and adults alike!

STEP 1

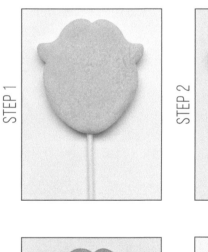

STEP 2

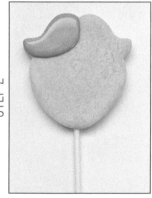

THE FINISHED LOOK

STEP 5

STEP 3

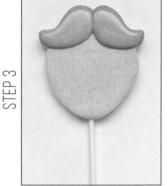

STEP 4

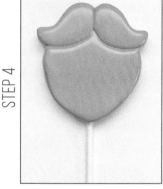

# POT O' GOLD

1. Outline the pot with black thick consistency icing and flood with black thin flood icing. Let dry for 20 minutes.

2. Outline and flood the feet of the pot using the same icings. Let cookie dry for at least 2 hours.

3. Outline and flood the top of the cookie with white medium flood icing.

4. Immediately sprinkle on your quins (round flat sprinkles) onto the entire white section. If you do not let your pot dry for long enough your sprinkles will stick to the pot as well. Let dry for 30 minutes.

5. Paint the quins with edible gold paint.

6. Add a handle to the pot using black piping consistency icing.

STEP 1

STEP 2

STEP 3

## THE FINISHED LOOK

STEP 4

STEP 5

STEP 6

# RAINBOW

1. Outline your cookie with white thick consistency icing and flood with white thin flood icing. Let dry for 30 minutes.

2. Splatter cookie with edible gold paint. Using red piping consistency icing, add the first stripe of the rainbow just inside of the border of the cookie.

3. Repeat this process with orange, yellow, green, blue, and violet piping consistency icing. Using the previous color as a guide and leaving a tiny bit of room so the colors do not touch or blend together.

STEP 1

STEP 2

## THE FINISHED LOOK

STEP 3

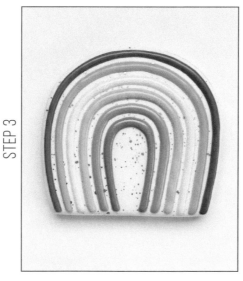

# NOTES

# EASTER

ICING COLORS: white, light pink, yellow, violet, light orange, orange
(add more orange gel color), green, sky blue, black

COOKIE SHAPES: carrot, chick, Easter egg, bunny

## CARROT

1. Outline and flood the carrot using orange medium flood icing. Leave a small section on the left side bare. This is an abstract effect so your bare section does not need to be a certain shape.

2. Immediately outline and fill the remaining bare section of the carrot with a light orange medium flood icing. Let dry for 20 minutes.

3. Add small lines onto either side of the carrot using orange piping consistency icing.

4. Outline and flood the leaves using green medium flood icing. Let dry for 15 minutes.

5. Outline the leaves using green piping consistency icing.

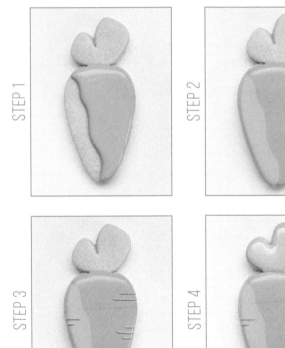

STEP 1

STEP 2

THE FINISHED LOOK

STEP 5

STEP 3

STEP 4

# CHICK

1. Outline egg shells with white thick consistency icing and flood with white thin flood icing. The cracked part of the egg is simply random zigzag lines. You might have noticed this about me by now but I like to make a lot of designs to where they can be piped in many different ways and still turn out beautiful! Let dry for 20 minutes.

2. Outline the sides of the chick with yellow thick consistency icing and flood the entire body with yellow thin flood icing. Use your scribe if necessary to get the icing into the cracks of the shell. Let dry for 30 minutes.

3. Add the eyes and beak using black and orange piping consistency icing. Add a small white dot to each eye using white piping consistency icing.

4. Outline the cracked section of the shell using white piping consistency icing.

5. Airbrush rosy cheeks using light pink airbrush color.

STEP 1

STEP 2

THE FINISHED LOOK

STEP 3

STEP 4

STEP 5

# EASTER EGG

1. Outline the entire cookie with sky blue thick consistency icing and flood with sky blue thin flood icing. Let dry for 30 minutes.

2. Add 3 stripes, one on the top, the middle, and the bottom of the egg. Use light pink piping consistency icing.

3. Add thin lines above and below each stripe using yellow piping consistency icing.

4. Add squiggly lines in the 2 middle sections using violet piping consistency icing.

5. Finish by adding dots into each curve of the previous section using light pink piping consistency icing.

*NOTE: Feel free to play around with your color combinations on this cookie!*

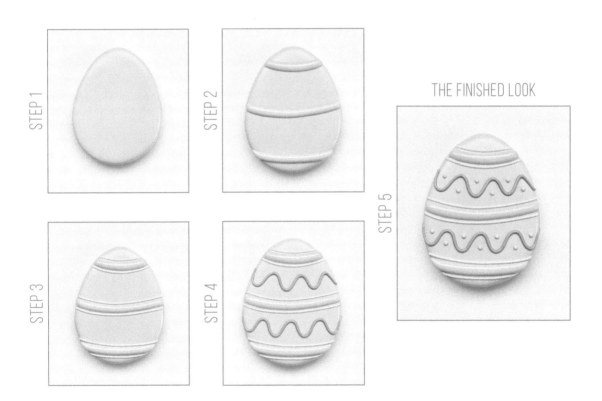

STEP 1

STEP 2

STEP 3

STEP 4

STEP 5

THE FINISHED LOOK

# BUNNY

1. Using light pink medium flood icing, paint the ears stopping just short of the border of the cookie. We will be covering the borders in the next step so the edges don't have to look pretty. Let dry for 10 minutes.

2. Outline the head and ears of the bunny with white thick consistency icing. Add tear drops onto the ears. Flood the head and the edges of the ears with white thin flood icing, leaving the inner ears so the pink shows through. Let dry for 15 minutes.

3. Outline the body with white thick consistency icing and flood with white thin flood icing. Let dry for 10 minutes.

4. Outline and fill the tail using white piping consistency icing. Use your scribe to swirl/fluff the tail.

5. Add a carrot to the center of the body using orange piping consistency icing. Let dry for 10 minutes.

6. Add 2 arms holding the carrot using white piping consistency icing. Add the leaves of the carrot using green piping consistency icing.

7. Add eyes and a nose using black and white piping consistency icing. Use your airbrush to add cheeks with light pink airbrush color.

STEP 1

STEP 2

STEP 3

STEP 4

STEP 5

STEP 6

STEP 7

## NOTES

_____

_____

_____

_____

_____

_____

_____

_____

_____

_____

_____

# MOTHER'S DAY

ICING COLORS: white, gray (a tiny bit of black gel color), green (green with a tiny bit of black gel color, dark green (more green with a tiny bit more black gel color), light pink, dusty rose (pink and violet gel color)

COOKIE SHAPES: pot, leaf 1, leaf 2, flower, flower cluster

## ———— FLOWER POT ————

1. Outline the bottom section of the pot using gray thick consistency icing and flood with gray thin flood icing. Let dry for 20 minutes.

2. Outline the lip of the pot using gray thick consistency icing and flood with gray thin flood icing. Let dry completely for 6–8 hours.

3. Use your scribe tool to etch horizontal and vertical lines into the icing.

STEP 1

STEP 2

THE FINISHED LOOK

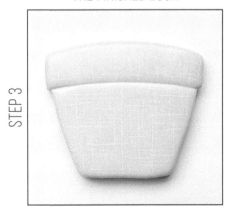

STEP 3

# LEAF 1

1.  Outline cookie with white thick consistency icing and flood with white thin flood icing. Let dry for 30 minutes.

2.  Pipe an outline just inside the border of the cookie and flood with green medium flood icing. Let dry for 20 minutes.

3.  Pipe a line down the middle of the cookie with green piping consistency icing. Add lines extending out from the center line at a diagonal to the end of the leaf.

STEP 1     STEP 2     STEP 3

# LEAF 2

1.  Outline entire cookie with white thick consistency icing and flood with white thin flood icing. Let dry for 30 minutes.

2.  Add a line down the middle of the cookie using dark green piping consistency icing.

3.  Outline leaves down one side of the stem using dark green piping consistency icing and fill with dark green medium flood icing. Let dry for 10 minutes.

4.  Outline and fill the leaves on the other side of the stem using dark green piping consistency and medium flood icing.

 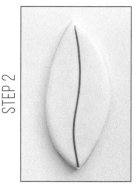  

STEP 1     STEP 2     STEP 3     STEP 4

# FLOWER

1. Add a blob of dusty pink thick consistency icing onto the center of the cookie using tip #103.

2. Using your dusty pink thick consistency icing and tip #103, begin piping petals around the blob by touching the piping tip to your cookie. As you squeeze the bag, lift the piping bag up and over the side of the blob at a 45 degree angle. Release pressure as you touch the piping tip back down to the cookie.

3. Repeat this step, overlapping the petals, about 5 times.

4. Near the edge of the cookie, touching the piping tip down to the cookie. As you begin squeezing, lift the piping bag and move the piping bag in small up and down motions a few times to create the first outer petal.

5. Continue this process 5–6 times around the cookie to create the outer layer of petals.

6. Add another layer of petals using this same technique, slightly overlapping the previous layer of petals.

7. Finish by adding a 3rd and final layer. Make sure to fill in the gaps between the 2nd layer of petals and the rose bud. If necessary use your scribe to move your icing around to fill in any remaining gaps.

STEP 1

STEP 2

STEP 3

STEP 4

STEP 5

THE FINISHED LOOK

STEP 6

STEP 7

# FLOWER CLUSTER

1. Pipe a stem on the left side of the cookie using dark green piping consistency icing. Add 5 leaves connecting to the stem using the same icing.

2. Pipe a stem on the right side using green piping consistency icing. To add the leaves to this section, start at the top larger section of the leaves. Pipe a bulb and as you slowly release pressure, drag the icing bag to connect to the stem.

3. With dusty rose thick consistency icing and tip # 103, add a rose to the top of the cookie using the same steps from the flower just before this cookie. Add only 2 layers of outer petals instead of 3.

4. Using tip #21 or any small star tip, start piping at the middle of the bottom left flower with light pink thick consistency icing.

5. Swirl the icing around the center about 2 times until you reach the edge of this section of the cookie.

6. Immediately sprinkle white nonpareils on this flower.

STEP 1

STEP 2

STEP 3

STEP 4

STEP 5

STEP 6

7. Add the last flower using white thick consistency icing using tip #103. Begin by touching the tip down to the cookie. As you squeeze the bag, slightly lift the bag above the cookie and move the bag up and down as you pipe around in a circle without stopping. It is easiest if you use a cookie swivel but if you are not using one you can use your hands to turn the cookie.

8. Repeat this process in the center, filling in the rest of the flower. If necessary use your scribe to fill in any gaps.

9. Add several small dots to the center using light pink piping consistency icing.

STEP 7

STEP 8

THE FINISHED LOOK

STEP 9

# FATHER'S DAY

ICING COLORS: tan (a touch of brown), brown, red, orange, yellow, green

COOKIE SHAPES: top bun, bottom bun, cheese, burger, lettuce, tomato

## ——— LETTUCE ———

1. Start at the edge of the cookie using green thick consistency icing and tip #104. Touch the tip of the bag to the cookie and lift slightly as you begin piping. Move the bag up and down as you make your way around the cookie.

2. You can continue around the cookie in one motion or stop to move the cookie by touching the tip back down to the cookie and releasing pressure.

3. Add another layer, slightly overlapping the first.

4. Add a third and final layer. Use your scribe to fill in any gaps.

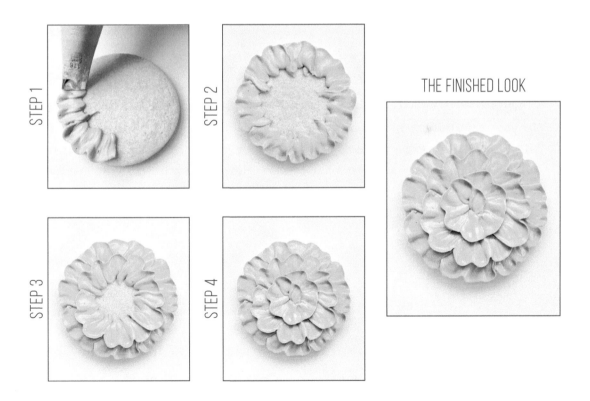

STEP 1

STEP 2

THE FINISHED LOOK

STEP 3

STEP 4

# CHEESE

1. Outline the cookie with orange thick consistency icing and flood with orange thin flood icing. Let dry for 15 minutes.

2. Airbrush the border of the cookie using orange airbrush color.

THE FINISHED LOOK

STEP 1

STEP 2

# BURGER

1. Outline and fill the entire cookie with brown thick consistency icing. Let dry for 5–10 minutes.

2. Use your scribe to break up the crust of the icing in a swirling motion. Let dry for 20 minutes.

3. Add the lines of the burger by holding your scribe horizontally and pushing the icing down.

4. Airbrush the border of the cookie and down the grill lines using an equal mixture of brown and black airbrush color.

THE FINISHED LOOK

STEP 1

STEP 2

STEP 3

STEP 4

# TOP BUN

1. Outline the cookie with tan thick consistency icing and flood with tan thin flood icing. Let dry for 30 minutes. Airbrush the border of the cookie using brown airbrush color.

2. Add sesame seeds using white piping consistency icing.

THE FINISHED LOOK

STEP 1

STEP 2

# BOTTOM BUN

1. Outline the entire cookie with tan thick consistency icing and flood with tan flood icing. Let dry for 30 minutes. Airbrush the border of the cookie using brown airbrush color.

2. Pipe a wavy line across the entire cookie using yellow piping consistency icing. Cut the tip of the bag larger to create a thicker line. Let dry for 10 minutes.

3. Pipe another wavy line over the "mustard" using red piping consistency icing.

THE FINISHED LOOK

STEP 1

STEP 2

STEP 3
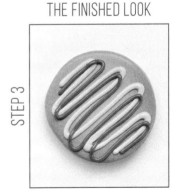

# TOMATO

1. Pipe a thin layer of red thin flood icing onto the center of the cookie, leaving the border of the cookie bare. Let dry for 30 minutes

2. Outline the cookie with red thick consistency icing. Pipe another line at the edge of your base layer. Mark the center of your cookie with a small circle and add 3 sections connecting the center to the outer circle. Flood these sections with red medium flood icing.

3. Add a smaller circle on top of the middle red circle using white thin flood icing.

4. Use your scribe to drag the icing from the center of the white circle out onto the dried base layer sections of the tomato.

5. Use your scribe to swirl the center of the tomato to further blend the red and white icing. If necessary, add a little extra white icing onto the center for more color contrast.

6. Add 3 seeds onto each section of the tomato using yellow piping consistency icing. Squeeze the piping bag to create the head of the seed. As you slowly release pressure, drag the piping bag down to the center of the cookie to create the seed shape.

STEP 1

STEP 2

STEP 3

THE FINISHED LOOK

STEP 4

STEP 5

STEP 6

# NOTES

# 4TH OF JULY

ICING COLORS: white, red, royal blue

COOKIE SHAPES: snow cone, bomb pop, flag, firework

## ——————— SNOW CONE ———————

1. Outline the cup of the snow cone with white thick consistency icing and flood with white medium flood icing. Let dry for 2 hours.

2. Outline the top dome with thick white consistency icing. Pipe red medium flood icing onto the left third of the cookie. Immediately pipe white flood icing in the middle section. Make sure the white icing is touching the red icing. Add blue medium flood icing onto the right section, filling in the rest of the bare cookie.

3. Sprinkle white sanding sugar onto the red white and blue icing. Gently shake off excess.

4. Use white piping consistency icing to outline the cup and add the seam across the middle.

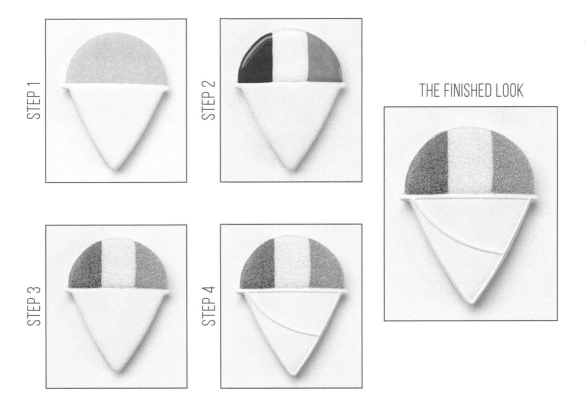

STEP 1

STEP 2

STEP 3

STEP 4

THE FINISHED LOOK

# BOMB POP

1. Add the stick of the popsicle using brown medium flood icing. Let dry for 20 minutes.

2. Outline the popsicle section of the cookie with white thick consistency icing. Divide the popsicle into thirds using the same icing.

3. Fill in the top section with red medium flood icing, the middle section with white medium flood icing, and the bottom with blue medium flood icing. Let dry for at least 2 hours.

4. Dab on white piping consistency icing onto the top right and bottom left of the popsicle with a paintbrush to create an ice crystal effect.

STEP 1

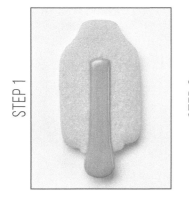

STEP 2

THE FINISHED LOOK

STEP 3

STEP 4

# FLAG

1. Using red thick consistency icing and tip #103, start with the tip touching the bottom corner of your cookie at a slight angle. As you begin piping, gently lift the bag up just enough so the tip is no longer touching the cookie. As you work your way around the border of your cookie, make tiny rainbows by moving the bag up and down as you move from one side to the other.

2. Using the same technique, pipe the next row of ruffles using white thick consistency icing and tip #103. Pipe this layer slightly overlapping the previous. Continue with a row of blue thick consistency icing and tip #103 slightly overlapping the white layer. Immediately sprinkle with red, white and blue nonpareils.

3. Repeat this process with your red white and blue thick consistency icing and tip #103. Finish with a red layer in the middle, or continue adding layers until you fill in the entire cookie. Use your scribe if needed to fill any gaps. Again, immediately sprinkle your new layers with red, white and blue nonpareils.

STEP 1

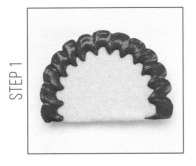

STEP 2

THE FINISHED LOOK

STEP 3

# FIREWORK

1. Outline the cookie with white thick consistency icing and flood with white thin flood icing. Let dry for 2 hours.

2. Airbrush stars onto your cookie using white airbrush color and spray with edible silver glitter while wet. Stencil is the Night Sky stencil from The Cookie Countess.

3. Pipe a small dot onto the center of the cookie using red medium flood icing. Pipe 2 tear drop shapes at the bottom of your cookie using red and blue medium flood icing. Use your scribe to drag the icing to a point towards the center of the cookie.

4. Continue adding different sized tear drop shapes around the side of the cookie, alternating colors.

5. Complete the other side of the cookie with your alternating tear drops shapes.

6. Pipe small dots in blank spaces around your cookie using your red and blue medium flood icing. Use your scribe to drag the icing to a point towards the center of your cookie.

7. Spray your firework with edible silver glitter.

STEP 1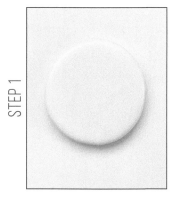

STEP 2

STEP 3

STEP 4

STEP 5

THE FINISHED LOOK

—— NOTES ——

# HALLOWEEN

ICING COLORS: white, orange, lime green (green and yellow gel color), violet, black

COOKIE SHAPES: bat, ghost, jack-o'-lantern, cauldron

## BAT

1. Outline and flood the wings with black medium flood icing.

2. Add small triangles onto the inner ears of the bat using black medium flood icing. Let dry for 15 minutes.

3. Outline the body and inner ears of the bat and flood with violet medium flood icing.

4. Add 3 lines to each wing with black piping consistency icing. Let dry completely for 6–8 hours.

5. Add 2 eyes using black and white piping consistency icing. Draw on the mouth and eyebrows using an edible black pen. Airbrush the cheeks using light pink airbrush color. *You can pipe the mouth and eyebrows on with black piping consistency icing if you do not have an edible pen. In this case, you only need to let the cookie dry for 15 minutes before adding the face.

STEP 1
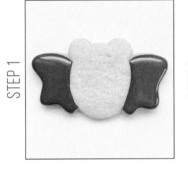

STEP 2

THE FINISHED LOOK

STEP 3

STEP 4

STEP 5

# GHOST

1. Outline the head and body of the ghost with white thick consistency icing and flood with white thin flood icing. Let dry for 20 minutes.

2. Outline the hands with white thick consistency icing and flood with white thin flood icing. Let dry completely for 6–8 hours.

3. Add 2 eyes using black and white piping consistency icing. Draw on the mouth and eyebrows using a black edible pen. Airbrush the cheeks using light pink airbrush color. *You can pipe the mouth and eyebrows on with black piping consistency icing if you do not have an edible pen. In this case, you only need to let the cookie dry for 15 minutes before adding the face.

4. Add a curved line from hand to hand using black piping consistency icing.

5. Add 3 upside down triangles onto the bottom of your black curved line using orange medium flood icing. Let dry completely for 6–8 hours.

6. Draw "BOO" onto the banner using an edible black pen (or pipe with black piping consistency icing). If you are using an edible pen, you can add the banner before you add the face so you only have to wait for one 6–8 hour period before drawing on the face and "BOO".

STEP 1
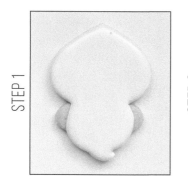

STEP 2

STEP 3

THE FINISHED LOOK

STEP 4

STEP 5

STEP 6
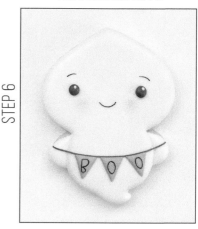

# JACK-O'-LANTERN

1. Using an icing scraper tool, scrape black medium flood icing onto the majority of your pumpkin. This will be the insides of the eyes and mouth so you do not need to cover the border of the cookie. Let dry for 15 minutes.

2. Outline the eyes and mouth using orange piping consistency icing. Feel free to have fun with different facial expressions!

3. Outline the left and right sections of the pumpkin using orange piping consistency icing. Be sure not to pipe inside of the eyes and mouth.

4. Flood both sections with orange medium flood icing. Let dry for 15 minutes.

5. Outline the top and bottom curves of the middle section and flood with orange medium flood icing. Try to carefully pipe on top of the lines of the mouth and eyes to create a more seamless blend.

6. Outline and flood the stem of the pumpkin using black medium flood icing.

7. Airbrush the border, seams, and around the eyes and mouth with orange airbrush color.

STEP 1

STEP 2

STEP 3

STEP 4

STEP 5

THE FINISHED LOOK

STEP 6

STEP 7
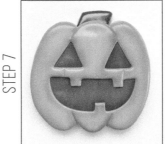

# CAULDRON

1. Outline the base of the cauldron with black thick consistency icing and flood with black thin flood icing. Let dry for 20 minutes.

2. Outline the rim and feet of the cauldron with black thick consistency icing and flood with black thin flood icing. Add an inner line of black thick consistency icing before flooding to help prevent cratering.

3. Outline a bone onto the middle of the cookie using white thick consistency icing and flood with white medium flood icing. Dry in front of a fan for 30 minutes.

4. Let's make some eyes for the witch's brew! On a piece of parchment paper, pipe 2 small circles using white medium flood icing.

5. Add another smaller circle using orange medium flood icing.

6. Finish by adding an even smaller circle using black medium flood icing and add 2 dots of white medium flood icing onto the black circle. Let dry in front of a fan to prevent cratering. These will take about 3 hours to dry. Try to be patient because taking them off too soon will make you sad. Don't ask me how I know that.

7. Add the "brew" onto the rest of the bare cookie using lime green thick consistency icing.

8. Use your scribe to swirl the icing. Add your eyeballs to the wet icing.

STEP 1     STEP 2     STEP 3

STEP 4     STEP 5     STEP 6

STEP 7

THE FINISHED LOOK

STEP 8

## ——— NOTES ———

# THANKSGIVING

ICING COLORS: white, red, orange, brown, yellow, black

COOKIE SHAPES: pumpkin pie, cherry pie, pecan pie, turkey

## —————— PUMPKIN PIE ——————

1.  There are not many things I enjoy more in the cookie world than a good cookie puzzle. See: Mother's Day and Father's Day on pages 73 & 79. Place your pie pieces together. If they are not fitting well, use a mircroplane grater to shave down the sides so they fit together better.

2.  Outline the pie piece with orange thick consistency icing and flood with orange thin flood icing. Leave a small section bare for the crust. Let dry for 20 minutes.

3.  Airbrush the border of the pie with orange mixed with brown airbrush color. Pipe a small dollop onto the center of the pie using white thick consistency icing and tip #16.

4.  To pipe the crust, start at the edge of the cookie with brown thick consistency icing and tip #103. Hold the bag as close to vertical as you can get. As you work your way across the cookie, move the piping bag up and down.

5.  Airbrush the crust with brown airbrush color.

STEP 1
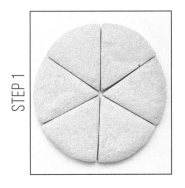

STEP 2

THE FINISHED LOOK

STEP 3
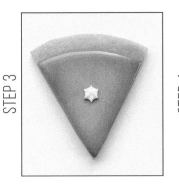

STEP 4
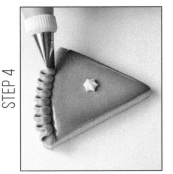

STEP 5
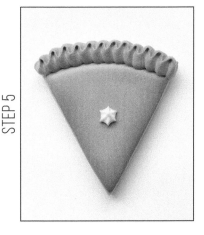

# CHERRY PIE

1. Pipe red circles onto your cookie with red piping consistency or medium flood icing. Leave room at the top for the crust. Make sure that these cherries are not touching. Let dry for 10 minutes.

2. Pipe more cherries, filling in some of the gaps, using red piping consistency or medium flood icing. Let dry for 10 minutes.

3. Fill in the rest of the gaps with your red icing. Let dry for 10 minutes.

4. Add lattice strips using brown thick consistency icing and tip #44.

5. Use the same crust technique from the pumpkin pie, and airbrush the crust using brown airbrush color.

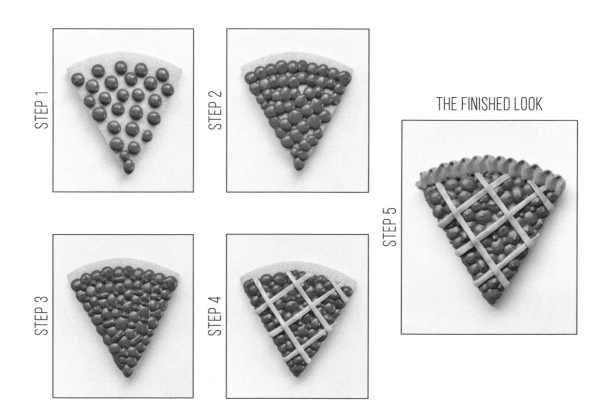

STEP 1    STEP 2    THE FINISHED LOOK

STEP 3    STEP 4    STEP 5

# PECAN PIE

1. Outline the pie with brown thick consistency icing and flood with brown thin flood icing. Leave room at the top for the crust. Let dry for 20 minutes.

2. Add the pecans using brown thick consistency icing and tip #16. As you begin squeezing the bag, push up slightly and then drag down. Slowly release pressure as you drag down.

3. Immediately sprinkle with white sanding sugar.

4. Use the same crust technique from the pumpkin and cherry pie, and airbrush the crust using brown airbrush color.

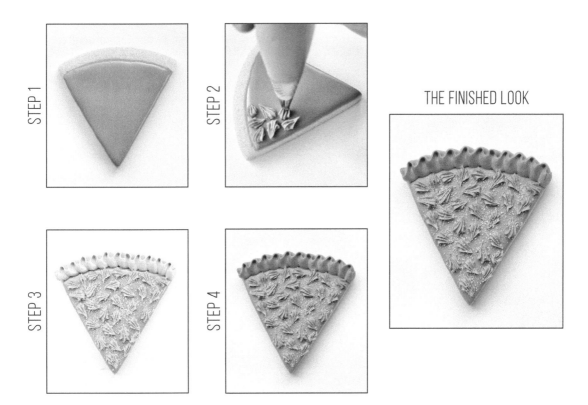

STEP 1

STEP 2

THE FINISHED LOOK

STEP 3

STEP 4

# TURKEY

1. Outline the body of the turkey with brown thick consistency icing and flood with brown thin flood icing. Let dry for 20 minutes.

2. Outline the wings with brown thick consistency icing and flood with brown thin flood icing. Add a blob of your thick consistency icing before flooding to help prevent cratering.

3. Outline and flood the beak and feet with orange medium flood icing. Let dry for 10 minutes.

4. Add the wattle using red piping consistency icing. Pipe on the eyes with black and white piping consistency icing. Draw on the eyebrows once the cookie is completely dry (6–8 hours) or pipe them on with black piping consistency icing.

5. Add the bottom feathers using yellow thick consistency icing and tip #70. To create the ruffled feather effect, push and pull the piping bag as you work your way to the tip of the feather keeping consistent pressure on the bag. Use your scribe to fill any gaps along the body.

6. Pipe the top feathers using the same technique with orange thick consistency icing.

7. Use your scribe or scraper tool to remove the bottom section that is overlapping where the middle feather will be.

8. Add the middle feathers using red thick consistency icing and tip #70. Use your scribe to fill in any remaining gaps.

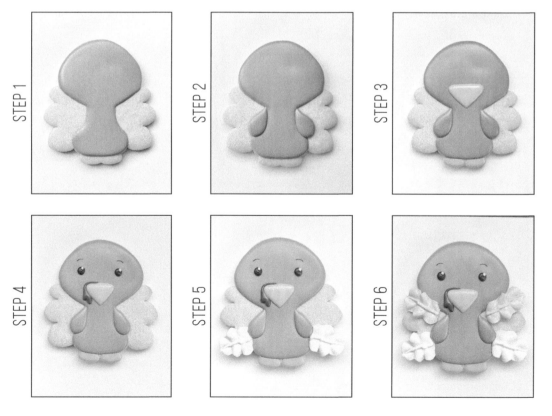

STEP 1 STEP 2 STEP 3 STEP 4 STEP 5 STEP 6

STEP 7

THE FINISHED LOOK

STEP 8

## NOTES

# CHRISTMAS

ICING COLORS: white, light pink, red, yellow, green, brown, dark brown, skin tone (start with a tiny amount of brown and pink, and add more brown for deeper skin tones), black

COOKIE SHAPES: candy cane, santa, reindeer, gingerbread house

## CANDY CANE

1. Outline the candy cane with white thick consistency icing. Add white stripes using the same icing.
2. Flood every other section with white thin flood icing.
3. Immediately fill in the remaining sections with red thin flood icing. Let dry for 20 minutes.
4. Outline the bow sections on the sides of the cookie with white thick consistency icing and flood with white thin flood icing. Let dry for 20 minutes.
5. Outline and flood the loops of the bow with green medium flood icing. Let dry for 15 minutes.
6. Add the tails of the bow with green medium flood icing. Let dry for 10 minutes.
7. Add the center circle of the bow using the same green icing.

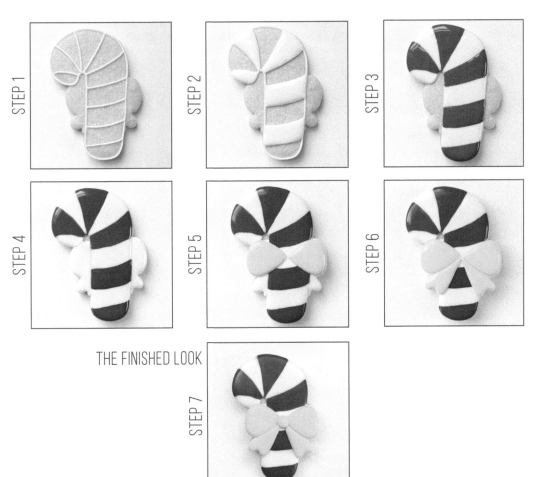

# SANTA

1. Outline and flood the beard using white medium flood icing.

2. Outline and flood the hat using red medium flood icing. Let dry for 15 minutes.

3. Fill in the face of the cookie using your choice of skin tone color medium flood consistency icing (the more brown gel color, the darker the skin tone). Let dry for 15 minutes.

4. Outline half of the mustache using white piping consistency icing, and flood with white medium flood icing. Let dry for 10 minutes.

5. Outline and flood the other half of the mustache using the same white icings. Let dry for 10 minutes.

6. Add the face using skin tone, black, and white piping consistency icing. Airbrush the cheeks using light pink airbrush color. Let dry completely for 6–8 hours.

7. Outline and fill the brim of the hat using white medium flood icing. Sprinkle on white sanding sugar and gently shake off the excess.

8. Outline and fill the pom-pom of the hat with white medium flood icing and sprinkle with white sanding sugar. Shake off the excess.

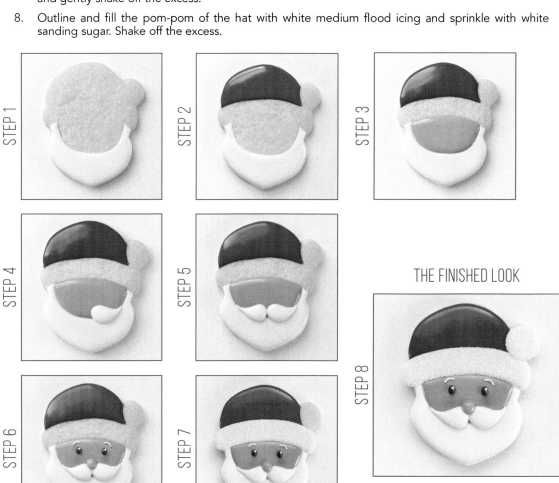

STEP 1 · STEP 2 · STEP 3 · STEP 4 · STEP 5 · STEP 6 · STEP 7 · STEP 8

THE FINISHED LOOK

# REINDEER

1. Outline and flood the head using brown medium flood icing.

2. Outline and flood the body using the same icing. Let dry for 15 minutes.

3. Outline and fill the other leg and tail using your brown medium flood icing.

4. Outline the ears and fill the bottom half using brown medium flood icing. Immediately fill in the other half with light pink medium flood icing.

5. Add the hooves using black piping consistency icing, and the collar using red medium flood icing. Let dry for 10 minutes.

6. Add 4 dots onto the collar using yellow piping consistency icing. Outline and flood the antlers using dark brown medium flood icing. Use your scribe to drag your icing into the corners if needed.

7. Using red, black and white piping consistency icing, add the nose and eyes. Use your edible black pen to draw on the mouth and eyebrows once your cookie is fully dry. Finally, Airbrush the cheeks using light pink airbrush color.

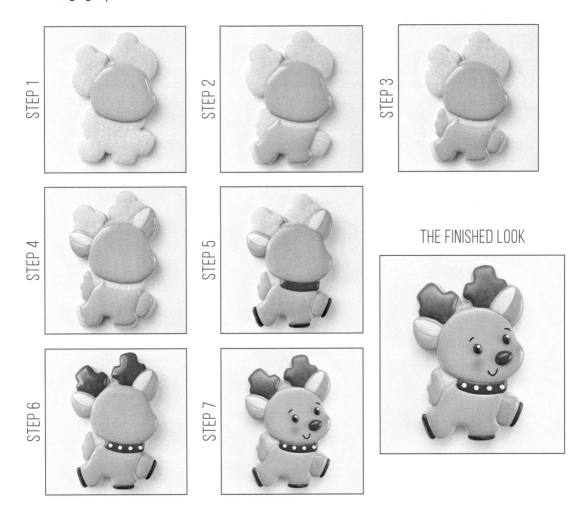

STEP 1 STEP 2 STEP 3 STEP 4 STEP 5 STEP 6 STEP 7

THE FINISHED LOOK

# GINGERBREAD HOUSE

1. Use a paintbrush to spread red thin flood icing onto either side of the bottom of the house. These will be the inside of the windows. Let dry for 10 minutes.

2. Outline the house using brown thick consistency icing. Outline the door and window and leave the candy canes on the side bare. Flood the entire cookie, except the door, windows and candy canes, with brown thin flood icing. Let dry for 20 minutes.

3. Fill in the door with red medium flood icing. Let dry for 10 minutes.

4. Outline the door and windows with white piping consistency icing. Add the window pains and doorknobs using the same icing.

5. Outline the candy canes with white thick consistency icing and flood in with white medium flood icing.

6. Immediately add stripes to the candy canes using red medium flood icing.

7. Outline snow on top of the house and chimney using white thick consistency icing and flood with white thin flood icing.

8. While the icing is wet, add your favorite Christmas sprinkles. I like to add the sprinkles one at a time so I have more control over the placement.

9. Add a wreath above the door using green piping consistency icing. Let dry for 10 minutes.

10. Add berries to the wreath using red piping consistency icing.

STEP 1

STEP 2

STEP 3

STEP 4

STEP 5

STEP 6

STEP 7

STEP 8

STEP 9

THE FINISHED LOOK

STEP 10

# NEW YEARS

ICING COLORS: white, gray, black

COOKIE SHAPES: NYE ball, clock, champagne bottle, "happy new year"

## NYE BALL

1. Outline cookie with gray thick consistency icing and flood with gray thin flood icing. Let dry for 30 minutes.

2. Add vertical lines using gray piping consistency icing, slightly curving the lines out to each side.

3. Add horizontal lines using gray piping consistency icing, slightly curving the lines towards the top and bottom.

4. Add 3 diamond sparkles using gray piping consistency icing. Use your scribe to drag out the points where necessary.

5. Airbrush the entire cookie with shimmer airbrush color and immediately spray with edible silver glitter.

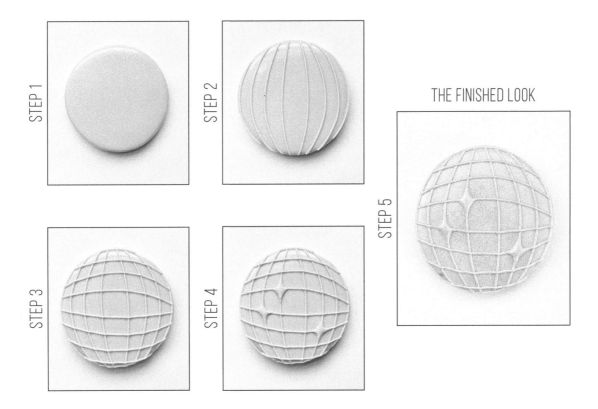

STEP 1

STEP 2

STEP 3

STEP 4

STEP 5

THE FINISHED LOOK

# CLOCK

1. Outline cookie with white thick consistency icing and flood with white thin flood icing. Let dry for 30 minutes.

2. Add the clock's roman numerals using black piping consistency icing. Start with 12, 6, 3 and 9 and then fill in the rest to make sure they are more evenly spaced out.

3. Add the hands of the clock using black piping consistency icing. Start with the center dot and pipe the hands up from that point.

4. Outline the cookie with black piping consistency icing.

STEP 1

STEP 2

THE FINISHED LOOK

STEP 3

STEP 4

# CHAMPAGNE BOTTLE

1. Outline and flood the top of the bottle with white medium flood icing. Let dry for 30 minutes.

2. Using a ball tool or the other end of a paintbrush, create dimples in the icing by lightly pressing the tool straight down into the icing.

3. Try not to push all the way down to the cookie, but if you do it's not the end of the world as we will be covering this part with paint! Let dry for 20 minutes.

4. Paint the icing with your choice of gold paint.

5. Outline the rest of the bottle with white thick consistency icing and flood with white thin flood icing. Let dry for 30 minutes.

6. Add the word "cheers" (or whatever you'd like it to say – the year for example) with black piping consistency icing. You can use a projector if you have one, or practice on wax/parchment paper before adding it to the cookie.

STEP 1

STEP 2

STEP 3

THE FINISHED LOOK

STEP 4

STEP 5

STEP 6

1. Outline cookie with black thick consistency icing and flood with black thin flood icing. Let dry for 30 minutes. Splatter the cookie with preferred edible gold paint or gold dust mixed with grain alcohol.

2. Add "happy" in the top middle of the cookie using white piping consistency icing.

3. Outline "new" using white piping consistency icing. Remember the wider sections of a letter are on the down stroke. Add an inner line on the down stroke sections with white piping consistency icing to prevent cratering. Again, you can use your projector or practice beforehand. You can even wait for the cookie to fully dry and etch the letter on with your scribe before piping.

4. Fill in the down stroke sections with white medium flood icing.

5. Repeat step 3 for the word "year."

6. If you haven't been drying in front of a fan I urge you to do so! Drying in front of a fan for the first 30 minutes will substantially reduce the risk of craters.

STEP 1

STEP 2

STEP 3

THE FINISHED LOOK

STEP 4

STEP 5

STEP 6

# NOTES

# WINTER

ICING COLORS: white, sky blue, dusty blue (sky blue with a touch of black), green, brown, orange, black

COOKIE SHAPES: snowman, tree, snowflake, hat

## — TREE —

1. Outline and flood the trunk of the tree using brown medium flood icing. Let dry for 10 minutes.

2. Using tip #21, start at the bottom corner of the cookie and pipe the first row of the tree. As you begin squeezing the bag, slightly push down and then pull up towards the top of the tree as you slowly release pressure.

3. Continue this technique until the bottom row is covered.

4. Add the rest of the rows of the tree, slightly overlapping the one previous. Finish at the top with a single "leaf" to create the point of the tree. Let dry full for 6–8 hours.

5. Add some snow throughout the tree using white piping consistency icing and immediately sprinkle with white sanding sugar. Shake off excess.

STEP 1

STEP 2

THE FINISHED LOOK

STEP 5

STEP 3

STEP 4

# SNOWMAN

1. Outline and flood the top and bottom snowballs with white medium flood icing. For the bottom snowball, add a curve on the top where the middle snowball will fit. Let dry for 20 minutes.

2. Outline and flood the middle snowball with white medium flood icing. Let dry for 20 minutes.

3. Add the face using black, white, and orange piping consistency icing. You can wait for the cookie to dry fully to add the eyebrows with a black edible pen or add it now with black piping consistency icing. Airbrush the cheeks using light pink airbrush color.

4. Add the arms using brown piping consistency icing, and the coal buttons using black piping consistency icing.

5. Using dusty blue piping consistency icing, pipe the scarf along the border of the top and middle snowballs. To create this effect, squeeze the bag to create a circle and as you slowly release pressure drag down and to the middle. Switch to the other side and repeat. The first 2 should look like a heart. Alternate sides each time until you reach the other side of the cookie.

6. Use this same technique to add the tails of the scarf. Add little tassels at the end using the same dusty blue piping consistency icing.

STEP 1
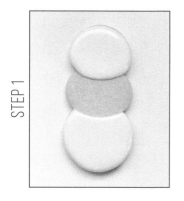

STEP 2
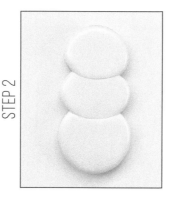

STEP 3

## THE FINISHED LOOK

STEP 4

STEP 5

STEP 6

# SNOWFLAKE

1. Outline and flood the longer points of the snowflake using blue medium flood icing.

2. Add the shorter points of the snowflakes using blue medium flood icing.

3. Use your scribe to drag the icing to a point in the middle. Let dry for 20 minutes.

4. Add lines through the middle of each section, and a small dot in the center using white piping consistency icing.

5. Add slightly angled lines extending from each center line using white piping consistency icing.

6. Pipe dots between each angled line. Start with larger dots on the outside and gradually pipe them smaller as you work your way into the center.

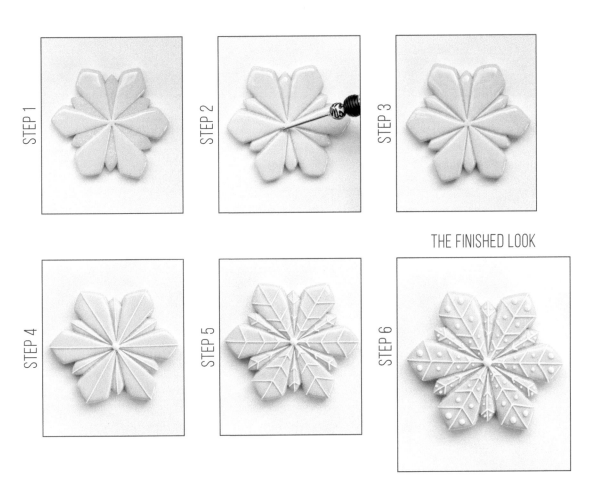

THE FINISHED LOOK

# HAT

1. Outline the head part of the hat with dusty blue thick consistency icing and flood with dusty blue thin flood icing. Try to add as little icing here as possible. We're aiming for dimension when we get to the folded part of the hat. Don't worry if your icing looks a little bit wavy, most of it will be covered here shortly! Let dry for 20 minutes.

2. Outline the bottom of the hat with dusty blue thick consistency icing and flood with dusty blue thin flood icing. Let dry for 30 minutes.

3. Add 2 slightly curved lines to the center of the hat using dusty blue piping consistency icing.

4. Working your way out from the middle, add 3 lines in a row, followed by a gap about as wide as the middle 2 lines you just piped. Continue this pattern until you reach the sides.

5. Using the same technique from the snowman, add the knit effect using dusty blue piping consistency icing. Start at the top and work your way down. Remember, you are essentially making tiny hearts, alternating sides with each stroke.

6. Add the knit pattern to each wide section until they are all filled.

7. Add lines straight down onto the fold of the hat, using the lines from above as a guide.

8. Repeat the knit technique to fill in the wide sections. Overlap the knit slightly onto the top section of the hat.

9. Add white thick consistency icing to the pom-pom.

10. Use a paintbrush and dab the icing to create a fur effect. You may have hand cramps now and for that I apologize, but you just made the cutest hat ever!

STEP 1  STEP 2  STEP 3  STEP 4  STEP 5  STEP 6

STEP 7

STEP 8

STEP 9

STEP 10

## THE FINISHED LOOK

# SPRING

ICING COLORS: white, pink, light pink, orange, tan, green, blue (royal blue gel color), dark blue (add more royal blue gel color)

COOKIE SHAPES: watering can, bird, flowers, sun hat

## FLOWERS

1. Outline entire cookie with white thick consistency icing and flood with white thin flood icing. Let dry for 30 minutes.
2. Add the 2 stems using green piping consistency icing. Outline and fill the leaves using the same icing.
3. Outline and fill the flowers with pink medium flood icing. Leave a circle in the center of each bare. Start outlining your flower at the stem to make sure the stem goes in between petals. Let dry for 15 minutes.
4. Add the centers of the flowers using light pink medium flood icing. Add lines down the center of the leaves using green piping consistency icing. Let dry for 10 minutes.
5. Finish with a swirl on the center of your flowers using light pink piping consistency icing.

STEP 1

STEP 2

THE FINISHED LOOK

STEP 3

STEP 4

STEP 5

# BIRD

1. Outline the body of the bird with blue thick consistency icing and flood with blue thin flood icing. Let dry for 30 minutes.

2. Outline and fill the tail feathers using a darker blue piping consistency icing. Use your scribe to drag the icing to a point if necessary.

3. Add the wing using a darker blue medium flood icing. Pro tip: complete the tails on all of your cookies first and thin out that icing a touch to use for the wings. Work smarter not harder am I right? Let dry for 20 minutes

4. Add the beak using orange piping consistency icing.

5. Outline the tail and wing with blue piping consistency icing.

6. Once the cookie is fully dry, draw on an eye using an edible black pen, or pipe it on right after step 5 with black piping consistency icing. Airbrush a cheek using light pink airbrush color.

STEP 1

STEP 2

STEP 3

THE FINISHED LOOK

STEP 4

STEP 5

STEP 6

# WATERING CAN

1. Outline and flood the middle of the watering can with green medium flood icing. Let dry for 15 minutes.

2. Add the handle and spout using green medium flood icing. Let dry for 10 minutes.

3. Add the sprinkler of the watering can with the same icing. Let dry for 10 minutes.

4. Pipe the 3 lines onto the main container and add the details onto the sprinkler with green piping consistency icing.

5. Add a daisy onto the center of the container using white piping consistency icing. Begin piping at the end of the petals and drag into the center as you slowly release pressure.

6. Finish with a small dot on the center of the daisy using pink piping consistency icing.

**STEP 1**

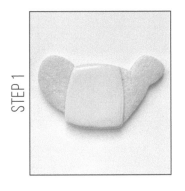

**STEP 2**

**STEP 3**

**STEP 4**

**STEP 5**

**STEP 6**

## THE FINISHED LOOK

# SUN HAT

1.  Outline the hat using tan thick consistency icing. Leave a small section in the middle bare for the ribbon. Flood both sections with tan flood icing. Let dry for 20 minutes.

2.  Fill in the ribbon section with light pink medium flood icing. Let dry for another 20 minutes.

3.  Outline the top and bottom sections of the hat using tan piping consistency icing. Starting from the center and working out, add lines from top to bottom onto both sections.

4.  Starting on one side of the cookie, add small horizontal lines over one of the vertical lines using tan piping consistency icing. Make sure to stop short of touching the next vertical line.

5.  Repeat this process for the next vertical line, offsetting the horizontal lines from the previous step so they fit together like a puzzle. Don't forget to add some tiny lines onto the very edge of the cookie, too!

6.  Continue this process for the rest of the vertical lines. Is now the time I should apologize again for the hand cramps?

STEP 1

STEP 2

STEP 3

THE FINISHED LOOK

STEP 4

STEP 5

STEP 6
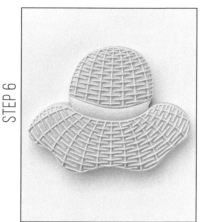

# NOTES

# SUMMER

ICING COLORS: white, red, pink, yellow, green, tan, black

COOKIE SHAPES: sun, watermelon, sandcastle, ice cream

## SUN

1. Outline the cookie with yellow thick consistency icing. Outline a circle in the middle of the cookie. Flood this section with yellow thin flood icing. Let dry for 30 minutes.

2. Fill in the circle with yellow thin flood icing. Let dry completely for 6–8 hours.

3. Add eyes and a mouth to the sun using an edible black pen and airbrush cheeks using light pink airbrush color.

STEP 1

STEP 2

THE FINISHED LOOK

STEP 3

# WATERMELON

1. Outline and flood the rind of the watermelon with green medium flood icing. Let dry for 15 minutes.
2. Airbrush the outer edge of the rind with green airbrush color.
3. Add a thin white stripe above the rind using white piping consistency icing. Let dry for 10 minutes.
4. Outline the rest of the watermelon with red thick consistency icing and flood with red thin flood icing. Let dry for 30 minutes.
5. Add seeds onto the watermelon using black piping consistency icing. Pipe a dot and drag down towards the tip of the watermelon as you slowly release pressure.

STEP 1  STEP 2  STEP 3  STEP 4  STEP 5  THE FINISHED LOOK

# SANDCASTLE

1. Use your scraper tool to add a layer of tan medium flood icing to the center of your cookie. Let dry for 30 minutes. It is important this part is dry so none of the sanding sugar in the next steps sticks to it.

2. Outline and fill the top and bottom of the sandcastle with tan medium flood icing.

3. Immediately sprinkle with white sanding sugar and shake off excess.

4. Outline the middle section, including a door above the bottom section. Flood with tan medium flood icing. Sprinkle with white sanding sugar and shake off excess.

STEP 1

STEP 2

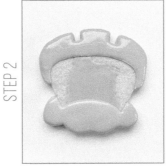

THE FINISHED LOOK

STEP 3

STEP 4

# ICE CREAM

1. Outline and flood the base of the cone with tan medium flood icing. Let dry for 15 minutes.

2. Outline and flood the top of the cone with tan medium flood icing.

3. Outline and flood the tops of each ice cream scoop with pink and white medium flood icing. Let dry for 20 minutes.

4. Outline both sections of the cone with tan piping consistency icing. Add diagonal lines onto the base of the cone.

5. Add diagonal lines going in the opposite way to the base of the cone using tan piping consistency icing.

6. Add the bottom of each ice cream scoop using pink and white piping consistency icing. Allow this part to crust over (dry) for 10 minutes.

7. Use your scribe to crush the surface of the icing.

STEP 1

STEP 2

STEP 3

STEP 4

STEP 5

THE FINISHED LOOK

# NOTES

# FALL

ICING COLORS: white, burgundy, orange, yellow,
dark teal (teal with a touch of black), brown

COOKIE SHAPES: pumpkin, mug, sunflower, sweater

## ──── PUMPKIN ────

1. Outline and flood the sides of the pumpkin with orange medium flood icing. Let dry for 15 minutes.

2. Outline and flood the middle section with orange medium flood icing. Let dry for 15 minutes.

3. Add lines down the center of each section, 2 for the middle section, using orange piping consistency icing.

4. Outline and fill the stem using brown piping consistency icing.

STEP 1
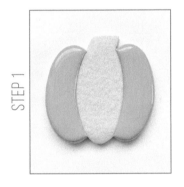

STEP 2

THE FINISHED LOOK

STEP 3

STEP 4

# MUG

1. Outline the mug with dark teal thick consistency icing and flood with dark teal thin flood icing. Let dry for 20 minutes.

2. Outline the handle of the mug with dark teal thick consistency icing and flood with dark teal thin flood icing. Let dry for 10 minutes.

3. Splatter cookie with white airbrush color, or white petal dust mixed with everclear.

4. Outline and flood the larger cinnamon stick with brown medium flood icing. Let dry for 15 minutes.

5. Outline and flood the other cinnamon stick with the same icing. Let dry for 15 minutes.

6. Outline the whipped cream with white thick consistency icing and flood with thin white flood.

7. Immediately sprinkle brown petal dust onto this section. Dip a paintbrush into the dust and gently tap the brush so the dust falls onto the wet icing.

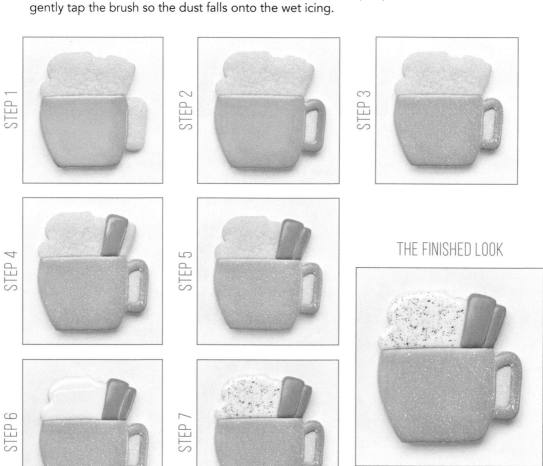

STEP 1 · STEP 2 · STEP 3 · STEP 4 · STEP 5 · STEP 6 · STEP 7

THE FINISHED LOOK

# SUNFLOWER

1. Using tip #104 and yellow thick consistency icing, pipe a petal onto the point of the flower. Slowly release pressure as you reach the tip of the petal.

2. Continue this technique for each point/petal.

3. Add another layer of petals using the same tip and icing. Pipe this layer in between the outer petals while also overlapping them.

4. Airbrush around the center of the petals using orange airbrush color.

5. Fill in the center with brown piping consistency icing. Let dry for 10 minutes.

6. Add small dots covering the center using brown piping consistency icing.

7. Airbrush the center using brown airbrush color. It's okay if some of the brown airbrush gets onto the petals. The more dimension the better!

STEP 1  STEP 2  STEP 3  STEP 4  STEP 5  STEP 6  STEP 7

THE FINISHED LOOK

# SWEATER

1. Outline the sweater leaving the bottoms and neck of the sweater bare using burgundy thick consistency icing. Flood with burgundy thin flood icing. Let dry for 20 minutes.

2. Outline the bottom sections and neck using burgundy thick consistency icing and flood with burgundy thin flood icing. Let dry for 20 minutes.

3. Outline the sweater, the bottom sections, and the neck using burgundy piping consistency icing. Add a line for the sleeves, and add vertical lines on the bottom sections and the neck.

4. Starting in the middle and working your way out, add vertical lines using the shape of the sweater as a guide with the burgundy piping consistency icing.

5. Add lines down the middle of every other section.

6. To create the cable knit, start at the top with a curved line using burgundy piping consistency icing. Cut the tip of the bag a little bit larger to make it easier.

7. Add another curved line going in the opposite direction, slightly overlapping the previous line. Continue this process down to the bottom of each section.

8. Add small dots onto every other small section using burgundy piping consistency icing.

STEP 1

STEP 2

STEP 3

STEP 4

STEP 5

STEP 6

STEP 7

STEP 8

THE FINISHED LOOK

—— NOTES ——

# INDEX

## NUMBERS

4TH OF JULY ............................................. 85

## A

AIRBRUSHING ........................................ 34

## B

BABY FEET ............................................. 44

BABY SHOWER ..................................... 43

BALLOONS .......................................... 50

BAT ..................................................... 91

BIB ...................................................... 43

BIRD ................................................... 122

BIRTHDAY ........................................... 49

BOMB POP .......................................... 86

BOTTOM BUN ...................................... 81

BUNNY ................................................ 70

BURGER .............................................. 80

## C

CAKE ............................................ 38, 52

CANDLE .............................................. 49

CANDY CANE ..................................... 103

CARROT .............................................. 67

CAULDRON .......................................... 94

CHAMPAGNE BOTTLE ......................... 111

CHEESE ............................................... 80

CHERRY PIE ......................................... 98

CHICK .................................................. 68

CHRISTMAS ......................................... 103

CLOCK ................................................. 110

## D

DOUBLE CHOCOLATE CHIP
   SUGAR COOKIES ............................. 25

DRESS .................................................. 39

## E

EASTER ................................................ 67

EASTER EGG ........................................ 69

ENVELOPE ........................................... 55

## F

FALL .................................................... 133

FATHER'S DAY ...................................... 79

FIREWORK ........................................... 88

FLAG ................................................... 87

FLOWER ............................................... 75

FLOWER CLUSTER ............................... 76

FLOWER POT ....................................... 73

FLOWERS ............................................. 121

FOUR LEAF CLOVER ............................. 61

## G

GHOST ................................................. 92

GINGERBREAD HOUSE ........................ 106

## H

HALLOWEEN ........................................ 91

"HAPPY NEW YEAR" ............................. 112

HAT ..................................................... 118

HEART ................................................. 56

## I

ICE CREAM .......................................... 130

## J

JACK-O'-LANTERN ................................ 93

## L

LEAF 1 ................................................. 74

# INDEX

LEAF 2 ............................................. 74

LEMON CARDAMOM SUGAR COOKIES ...... 21

LEPRECHAUN BEARD ..................................... 62

LETTUCE ............................................. 79

LOVE BUG ............................................. 57

## M

MONOGRAM ............................................. 40

MOTHER'S DAY ............................................. 73

MUG ............................................. 134

## N

NEW YEARS ............................................. 109

NYE BALL ............................................. 109

## O

OUTLINING AND FLOODING ...................... 32

## P

PAJAMAS ............................................. 45

PARTY HAT ............................................. 51

PECAN PIE ............................................. 99

POT O' GOLD ............................................. 63

PUMPKIN ............................................. 133

PUMPKIN PIE ............................................. 97

## R

RAINBOW ............................................. 64

RATTLE ............................................. 46

REINDEER ............................................. 105

RING ............................................. 37

ROSE ............................................. 58

ROYAL ICING ............................................. 29

## S

SANDCASTLE ............................................. 129

SANTA ............................................. 104

SHORTBREAD CUTOUT COOKIES ............... 27

SNOW CONE ............................................. 85

SNOWFLAKE ............................................. 117

SNOWMAN ............................................. 116

SPRING ............................................. 121

ST. PATRICK'S DAY ............................................. 61

STRAWBERRY LEMONADE
SUGAR COOKIES ............................................. 23

SUMMER ............................................. 127

SUN ............................................. 127

SUNFLOWER ............................................. 135

SUN HAT ............................................. 124

SWEATER ............................................. 136

## T

THANKSGIVING ............................................. 97

TOMATO ............................................. 82

TOP BUN ............................................. 81

TREE ............................................. 115

TURKEY ............................................. 100

## V

VALENTINE'S DAY ............................................. 55

VANILLA SUGAR COOKIES ............................................. 19

## W

WATERING CAN ............................................. 123

WATERMELON ............................................. 128

WEDDING ............................................. 37

WINTER ............................................. 115

# ABOUT THE AUTHOR

JOY CORTS is the cookie artist behind Joy of Baking. Joy began decorating cookies in late 2016. What started out as a hobby, making cookies for friends and family, quickly turned into creating tasty treats for strangers. In 2018 Joy left her career as a Kindergarten teacher to pursue cookie decorating full time and is now well known in her community as the cookie lady. Whether it's a baby shower, birthday or wedding, people return to her to help make their day extra special. Aside from creating custom cookies for her local customers and surrounding businesses, she keeps nothing a secret. When Joy is not making cookies, she enjoys spending time with her 2 kids and husband swimming in their pool, walking at local nature trails and going on adventures to new places around town.